21 days to the Perfect Dog

The friendly boot camp for your imperfect pet

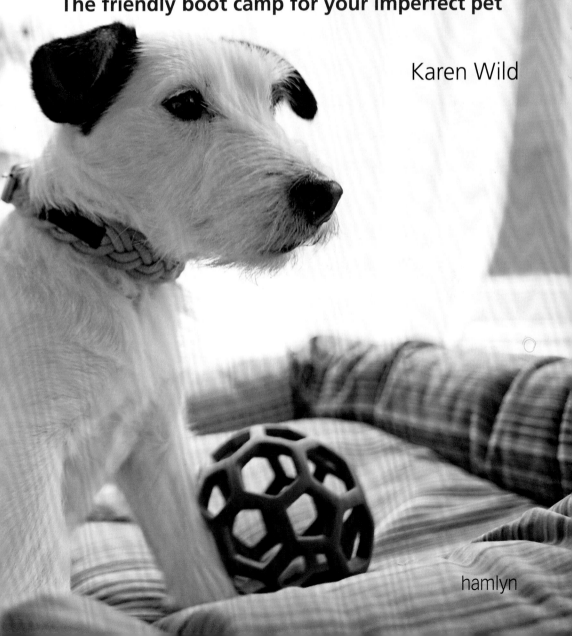

21 days to the Perfect Dog

The friendly boot camp for your imperfect pet

Karen Wild

hamlyn

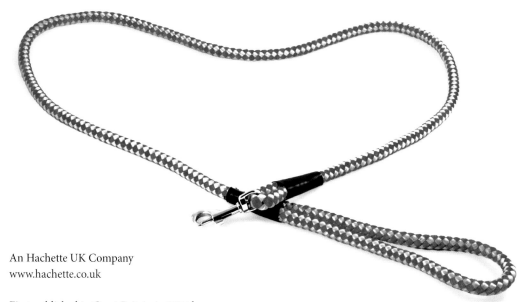

An Hachette UK Company
www.hachette.co.uk

First published in Great Britain in 2014 by
Hamlyn, a division of Octopus Publishing Group Ltd
Endeavour House
189 Shaftesbury Avenue
London
WC2H 8JY
www.octopusbooks.co.uk

Karen Wild asserts the moral right to be identified as
the author of this work

ISBN 978-0-600-62595-7

A CIP catalogue record for this book is available from
the British Library

Printed and bound in China

10 9 8 7 6 5 4 3 2 1

Disclaimer

The advice in this book is provided
as general information only. It is not
necessarily specific to any individual
case and is not a substitute for the
guidance and advice provided by
a licensed veterinary practitioner
consulted in any particular situation.
Octopus Publishing Group Ltd
accepts no liability or responsibility
for any consequences resulting
from the use of or reliance upon the
information contained herein.

Unless the information given in this
book is specifically for female dogs,
dogs are referred to throughout
as 'he'. The information is equally
applicable to both male and female
dogs, unless otherwise specified.

Contents

Part 1:
Assessment

Everything you need to know before starting to train

Introduction

Welcome to the friendly 'obedience boot camp', our 21-Day Training Plan for your dog. It is filled with fun exercises that will help you bond with your dog and turn your canine friend into an even greater companion. It will guide you through assessing your dog's skills, to step-by-step training of every core skill your dog will ever need, and provide troubleshooting solutions for any problem areas.

This book is ideal for dogs at all stages of their lives and learning, so whether you have just said 'Hello!' to a new puppy or an older dog, the 21-Day Plan is ideal if you are looking for day-by-day encouragement and guidance. It will keep you on track, no matter how busy your everyday routine is at the moment. Of course, all training requires you to make changes to existing habits, but we have made this as simple as possible with an easy-to-follow format. Every step is explained in full and illustrated in photographs to help you gain an instant understanding of what to do and what to expect as your dog learns each new skill.

Easy learning for greater sociability

Our methods are positive, reward-based, and fair, but you will find that all behaviour boundaries are securely maintained. Your dog will learn in a structured way that protects his welfare and keeps things clear and simple.

Your family can get involved, too, as your dog builds up his new skills. Dogs are social animals, but they need training to make sure that whether they are socializing with other dogs, children or adults, there are rules that need to be obeyed. This is so important, for his happiness and your own, that we have included many sections on socialization, covering all areas of his life, to encourage him to stay calm and relaxed in even the most challenging situations.

Karen Wild

There is no need to delay. Why not begin the 21-Day Training Plan right now? You and your dog are going to have fun!

How to get started

This first section has been designed to help you assess your dog's current level of learning and decide how much, or how little, your dog can learn each day. It will also help you to assess your own level of teaching skill and find out how you can become a better, more effective teacher. Once you have made your assessments, keep them in mind as you and your dog progress through the 21–Day Training Plan.

Set the right pace

As you start assessing your dog, you will learn about the expectations you have for him, taking into account his different life stages and abilities, as well as his breed instincts. This will result in well-taught, individualized lessons, and in 21 days you will have a keen dog that has bonded closely with you and the rest of the family.

Your home life is important, and although the 21-Day Plan will ask you to set aside time each day for training your dog, you will find that it is possible to set and achieve realistic goals within your family lifestyle. Simply adapt the schedule to fit your family's, your own, and your dog's needs.

A new approach to training

Training pushes forward your dog's existing level of ability to a new level, so it is inherently challenging. This 'fun boot camp' takes a light approach but it is based on a serious foundation. In this first section you will find an explanation of all the core training theories that lie behind the 21-day course, together with an examination of the typical issues surrounding canine obedience. Every exercise needs to be completed with love and patience: willing dogs are obedient dogs.

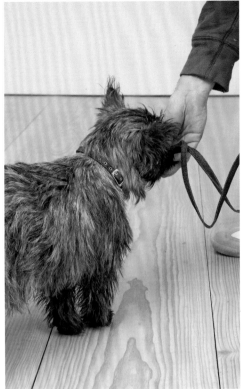

Never push your dog too hard and always stop your training sessions long before he becomes tired or stressed. During the plan, you are actively encouraged to work in brief sessions (usually of five to ten minutes), and new learning skills are interspersed during the day with regular recaps on skills learned earlier. The timeline at the beginning of each day plan shows you exactly what you and your dog will be doing that day. But don't think that you have to do this alone – involve your family and everyone else who might come into contact with your dog.

Core training skills

The 21-Day Plan focuses on positive, reward-based methods as used by modern dog professionals. There is clear evidence that these methods are the least stress-inducing and fairest ways to teach any animal. There will still be boundaries, and you will still have control when it is needed. Nevertheless, be confident that the plan teaches core obedience skills in a kind and effective way.

'Free choice' sections

From Day 4 you will see special sections called 'Free choice'. These are suggestions for ways to look again at an activity of your own choice. They are interspersed throughout the 21-Day Plan to give you and your dog a chance to revise something that you feel needs a little more practice or to simply enjoy a relaxing, sociable activity instead. In all training, pacing your progress is an important teaching skill. Take advantage of 'Free choice' to ensure your dog's welfare, giving him plenty of time to recoup his energy and so maintain enthusiasm. You might find yourself keen for a rest too – or you might be just as keen as your dog to practise rolling a ball a few more times!

Become the expert on your own dog

Once you have completed this section, you will be well-informed about your own dog and the things that motivate dogs in general. You will have rehearsed the handling skills you need and will be ready to begin the 21-Day Plan.

New beginnings

Before you embark on the 21-Day Plan, you need to consider the issues that may come up in the training of dogs at different life stages, especially when they all have varying past experience.

Before you start, make sure your dog has had a thorough veterinary health check, so you can take into account any physical issues before commencing the programme.

Existing habits

The first thing you need to assess is your dog's current habits, as these will affect future training. Have you allowed your dog to jump up at you in the past? Has he learned any unwanted behaviours in a different home? You will need extra practice and patience to teach him a new, alternative behaviour. You and he will both need to be patient – while your dog is learning new habits from the 21-Day Plan, the best way to maintain boundaries

of acceptable behaviour is by anticipating and preventing not only your dog's mistakes, but your own, too. Always avoid harsh punishment when errors inevitably occur, and act with kindness.

Life stages

Life stages and past experience have an impact upon learning speed and retention, and on energy levels. Is your dog a new puppy, an adolescent (aged from 6 months to 18 months, approximately), or a fully-grown adult? If he is a rescue dog, is it possible to find out more about his background history?

Teaching a puppy

If you have a puppy under 12 weeks of age, concentrate your efforts on socializing him thoroughly. See the 'Socialization progress chart' on pages 92–93. The 21-Day Training Plan is designed to complement this process once your puppy is over 12 weeks of age, so start there and just practise his socializing skills until he is at least 12 weeks old.

Puppies are enthusiastic, but their energy can be misleading. You will need to adapt the 21-day programme to incorporate additional rest periods throughout the day, to allow him to recoup his mental and physical energy. If he begins mouthing, stealing, or racing around madly, he is probably overtired or overstimulated. Slow your pace and add in more frequent breaks.

Your puppy may also be awaiting his final vaccinations when you begin this book, so continue the 21-Day Plan at home and in your garden, but still carry him out and about to allow socialization to continue.

Helping rescue dogs

Rescue dogs sometimes undergo stressful experiences before rehoming. Your rescue dog may have already been partially trained or may have learned not to trust people or other dogs. Make a note of learned behaviours he performs that you have not yourself taught. You can build on this later on in the programme by changing them into behaviours you prefer.

Give your rescue dog a period of time to settle in and get to know you before you start the 21-Day Plan. Then teach him as if he were a new puppy. Offer him chances to learn that previous owners may not have provided, and aim for steady, sure, and slow progress. Focus on building trust and be prepared to let him retreat when he needs to. If he is tired or shows signs of stress, remember that you can always re-start the training on another day.

Adult dogs

If you have an adult dog that you have owned since puppyhood, he will be ready for a 21-Day refresher – so unless you feel he has particular needs, you will not need to adapt the plan a great deal. List any learned habits that are not welcome. Follow the instructions step by step, and consult the troubleshooting section as necessary, to help you both quickly establish some more desirable patterns of behaviour. Use the 21-Day Plan to forge a brand new path towards new skills, thoroughly taught, and consistently rewarded. This creates simplicity for your adult dog and builds a trusting bond.

Elderly dogs, new skills

Given time, even elderly dogs can learn new skills. Training is a gentle way to reintroduce familiar and rewarding routines into an elderly dog's life. Start the 21-Day Plan more gradually – perhaps taking two days to complete one day's tasks, at first, until you can gauge your dog's preferred pace. Give him extra practice at each stage to aid retention of skills, and frequent breaks. Your dog will still feel a sense of bonding and achievement when he earns the rewards on offer.

Step-by-step teaching will help him to rely on a safe and reliable routine, at a time when physical aspects of his well-being may be declining through old age. Take account of any health issues he may have, and ask your vet to check for signs of cognitive decline before you attempt new learning. Further help on owning an elderly dog can be found in the '50 Quick Fixes' section (see pages 66–91).

Setting targets

Once you have carried out a basic assessment of your dog's training needs – in terms of age, background history, and temperament – you will begin to have a better idea of what to expect from him during training. Your expectations need to be realistic; high expectations lead to impatience and create excessive pressure on both you and your dog. This is unproductive as it reduces enjoyment and suppresses learning. Have a day off if the pace of the plan seems too rapid. Remember that this is true for you as much as for your dog: if you are no longer having fun, he will sense it, and the training will not be as effective.

As long as you keep up regular practice, and have fun with your dog while teaching him, the bond between you will strengthen and the training will get done. If you do need to take a day off, simply return to the plan when you both feel rested and ready to get going again.

Keeping track

The best way to measure progress is to set targets, and the 21-Day Plan helps you to do just that. Each day of the plan starts with a timeline to remind you of what to do each day. Some tasks are new, while others will be recapping on skills learned earlier, to reinforce them in your dog's memory. Follow the order and time limits given in the day's timeline. You can also use the checklist included at the back of the book to assess just how far you have both progressed, which is a great way to stay motivated.

While you and your dog are working through the 21-Day Plan, your teaching environment may not match the distractions of an everyday setting, but you will progress to this. For instance, you may be teaching him mainly in your home, which may or may not be home to other people or other animals – it may have lots of distractions or very few. This is nothing to be concerned about, because the skills you are teaching him will translate into other areas, such as a park, when you need them to. In the meantime, teaching your dog to come back to you, for instance, can be used to move him from the sofa, stop him chasing cats, or prevent him from jumping up at visitors.

Practical applications

As you teach each exercise from the 21-Day Plan, think about how you could use this training in other circumstances. In what situations might it be useful to be able to ask him to 'Come'? What other applications can you think of for 'Fetch'? If possible, try to vary the environment, setting up situations such as meeting strangers, so that your dog can really practise the skill. Remember that a new situation will always be more difficult at first, so set your target slightly lower each time you change the situation.

Form a lifelong habit

Training must continue beyond the 21-Day Plan if all the good work you have put into it is to develop into an everyday response. After you have finished the plan, continue to set aside time each day to work with your dog, and keep it in place for the future. Even if the time is spent playing a retrieve game or grooming him, this special contact with your dog is essential to maintain the new habits.

Once your dog has learned the basic skills, it is your job to work these into his normal routine. Use 'Sit' and 'Stay' at his mealtimes, and 'Wave' when greeting people. Keep focused, particularly when on walks, and do not let bad habits such as pulling on the lead creep in. If ever you and your dog fail to work well as a team, stop, assess the situation, and revisit the 21-Day Plan. Never be afraid to change something you are doing to help your dog learn, even if this means returning to a simpler stage of training for a time.

Family involvement

Your dog is part of the family, and everyone in your household will want to help him learn. Apart from the fun in teaching him new skills, it's also a great way to get to know him better. From a safety point of view, people in regular contact with your dog also need to know how to control him, with kindness and in ways that he can understand. Their ways and your ways must be consistent, or your dog will become confused. Communicate each day's training to others using the straightforward format of the 21-Day Plan.

Who teaches the dog?

Decide who will take overall responsibility for your dog's training. Dogs are versatile animals and form relationships with lots of individuals with whom they regularly interact, and the type of relationship they build depends on what they learn from these interactions. Do not feel discouraged

or surprised if your dog responds better to some people than others. Explain to everyone involved that this is part of the learning process as the dog works out who is easiest to understand, or who gives rewards out more freely!

Some years ago, many people thought that dogs were pack animals who fell into acknowledged ranks, with one dog taking the position of 'alpha' or 'top dog'. Some trainers believed that it was important for every dog owner to establish firmly that he or she was 'top dog' in their relationship. However, research has shown that dogs do not set up packs; nor do they have any sense of a hierarchy within their environment. Studies have also shown that dogs learn in order to please their owners, so reward-based training, as used in the 21-Day Plan, is the most effective way to train. One older idea that might be worth bearing in mind is that your role is that of the 'guardian' –

someone who will look out for your dog, teach him, and maintain responsibility for his actions at all times.

When can others join in?

The best way to put the 21-Day Plan into action is for you to train your dog in each new skill to a reasonable level, before allowing others to teach under your supervision. This keeps confusion to a minimum and sets a clear boundary for your dog regarding your position and others in your household. You are the training 'expert' for your dog – do not be swayed by others' methods, which may be based on inexpert advice, and do not let other methods or people interfere with the bonding that will take place following adherence to the complete 21-Day Plan.

Exercising caution around children

Children will need detailed coaching from you on how to work with your dog. If they are excluded from joining in the 21-Day Plan, they may attempt some impromptu training when you are not there to supervise. There are certain things to bear in mind when allowing children near your dog:
● A rescue dog or older dog may not welcome such contact, so maintain calm but strict boundaries for children's behaviour.
● Children cannot easily read stress signals in dogs (see page 70).

Be especially vigilant when children are around your dog and teach them to allow your dog to retreat when he chooses.
● Never allow children to disturb your dog while he is resting.
● Well-behaved children can still be bitten when trying to show affection by hugging or stroking.
● As long as your dog is well-socialized, children and dogs form a strong bond. Part of the training is to make sure that he will not be fazed by children's high-pitched voices and jerky movements.

You might like to enrol children's help in planning sessions, or allow them to assist you by collecting items that are needed for training. However, only permit a child to become involved with the training plan when you are confident that your dog is relaxed in his or her presence.

Enlisting help from visitors

By all means encourage visitors to help you work through the 21-Day Plan socialization sections; they can also assist with training an excitable dog to sit, for example. However, make sure that you always take control of these sessions and show them the plan, so that they can follow your approach. Never allow anyone to play roughly or behave in a heavy-handed manner with your dog, as this only undermines the trust and gentleness you are working hard to build.

Keeping things fun

Although it is a 21-day programme, this plan does not have to be followed in an intensive three-week stretch. Instead it can be a longer stretch with plenty of breaks between the official 'training days'. Give yourself and your dog time to learn and this way, you will keep the enjoyment factor high!

Learning through play

Enjoyable experiences are highly memorable, so while keeping to the formal schedule of the training plan, make the sessions informal and light-hearted. You can be confident that both you and your dog will always learn something new, even if it is not the task you have planned! Your dog is learning about how you interact with him, while you are learning how he responds to your methods and assessing his needs as you train.

If you feel relaxed, your dog will relax too, so choose a time of day when you are both feeling calm. Keep your voice light and happy.

Short sessions maintain motivation

In each day of the 21-Day Plan, the sessions are timed in short bursts, of five or ten minutes. This is to ensure energy levels and motivation remain high during training, so even if things are going well, stop when your time is up.

There are a few key things to remember:
- Keep your dog always wanting more, so he begins each training session with enthusiasm.
- Older and sensitive dogs will show renewed interest if you begin with very short, easy sessions that can be increased in intensity over time.
- Excitable dogs need focus, so lower your voice and keep a steadier pace to aid concentration.

● Puppies may appear to be full of energy, but that energy is usually only available to them in short bursts. They will need regular rest periods, so be sure to build them into your training sessions. Excessive mouthing is usually a sign of overtiredness or overstimulation.

Low pressure, low risk.

Your dog is learning a new training 'language' that is designed to preempt problems in the home and when you take him into urban areas or parks. Teaching him skills before he actually needs them is better than waiting for problems to occur and then trying to resolve them. It is important for your dog to learn new skills when you and he are relaxed – this will guarantee that his new learning will not be smothered by frustrating errors, and your teaching will not become fraught.

While training, keep confusion to a minimum, and remain good-humoured if things go awry. You will not be able to control every element of the environment while training, and sometimes you will need to cope with unexpected events. If you are training in a park, there is always the possibility of major distractions – both human and canine – that will make it harder for your dog to concentrate. If you have made several attempts to teach something and your dog simply does not understand what you expect from him, take a break and review your training method and mood. It is probably your handling that is failing; if you are distracted or tired, you may be unable to communicate effectively to your dog.

If you have made errors in handling, the low-pressure approach of the plan means that any damage is limited. Thankfully, dogs are very forgiving! Simply start that day's training again on the following day, and mark the lost day down to experience.

End on a good note

You and your dog need time to review each day's teaching. 'Latent learning' is learning that occurs when the brain reviews information while occupied doing other everyday things. Make sure you end each session with a successful outcome, and resist the temptation to have another go there and then. When you return to training, you will find that only a brief reminder will indicate that your dog really has learned a great deal in your short session, even if you thought the session had not gone particularly well.

Rewards and signals

The 21-Day Plan uses reward-based training, so understanding how rewards work is essential to teaching your dog effectively. This means that you will need to identify what he finds enjoyable – what he counts as a 'treat' – before you begin.

Finding a reward to suit your dog

The training plan uses food, toys, or petting your dog as rewards. Get to know which rewards your dog likes best, but be careful not to increase his overall food intake through introducing too many delicious food treats. Note the following points regarding the different types of rewards:

● Food treats – these should be simple to handle, such as small pieces of food. Choose soft, strongly scented food such as cheese, ham, chicken, liver or sausage. Check that none of these will upset your dog's diet, and use his favourite whenever possible.

● Toys – these should fit in your pocket, so that you can easily take them along on walks, and they

must be easy for your dog to pick up. Toys made from fabric that you can wiggle about (pretending that they are 'alive') are best for dogs with low motivation, because the wriggling movement makes them irresistible.

● Petting your dog as a reward is useful, but do check that your dog is actually enjoying it. Some dogs will tolerate touch, but tend to move rapidly away rather than come back for more.

'Life' rewards

Dogs value freedom to do certain things and explore their environment in certain ways. This includes:

● Sniffing
● Foraging
● Novelty (new people, dogs, or places)
● Making eye contact
● Playing with other dogs
● Excited movement

● High-pitched noises, such as a lifted voice or squeaky sounds.

It is a good idea to adopt these more subtle, 'lifestyle' preferences as rewards rather than treats and toys as your training progresses. For example, you could begin to teach your dog that his reward for sitting and looking at you calmly is to play with other dogs. He will soon be happy to give you his full attention for short periods of time.

Make a reward valuable

Older or rescue dogs may not respond strongly to any reward. If this is the case with your dog, it may be because rewards have been incorrectly used on him in the past, and he no longer sees them as something worth having. However, you can increase the value of your chosen rewards, particularly food. On the basis that all dogs need to eat, a hungrier dog will be more motivated to work for food, so he will value a food treat more highly. Dogs are often given the same food every day, which decreases its value, so ensure that their special 'training food' is something they rarely get. Also remember that a strongly scented, fresher food – such as small pieces of meat or cheese – will stimulate a dog's nose and encourage him to seek out how best to earn it.

To make toys more valuable to your dog, choose a soft, squeaky toy that wiggles about when moved. Keep this toy out of reach and only use it for training. Choose times when your dog is lively and excitable for toy training, such as when you have just arrived home. This will ensure that he gives you his full attention, is engaged, and ready for some fun.

Fading out frequent rewards

Once your dog is competent at a skill, you can give him less-exciting rewards. Reduce their value by using food that is slightly less tasty than normal or a quieter, rubber toy instead of a squeaky one that rolls around. Only decrease the toy value once you are confident that your dog enjoys the activity he is performing or is doing it out of habit. Always offer some kind of reward to motivate him – if someone stopped paying you wages, you would stop working too!

Reward yourself

The 21-Day Plan is a team effort, so give yourself a bonus for completing each day's tasks, even if this is only congratulating yourself on having taken another step towards a happier family pet. You need to keep yourself movtivated too!

Trainer skills

Before beginning the 21-Day Plan, you need to familiarize yourself with the learning process, so you can operate as an effective trainer. This section helps you to understand and practise important facts about training and skills that you need to know before starting to teach your dog.

The mechanics of training

Your dog will need to be focused on how he can earn the reward on offer (see the section on 'Rewards' on pages 18–19 for suitable ones). Make yourself familiar with the following aspects of training:

Lures

A lure is used to attract your dog into a position or behaviour you would like him to adopt. A lure usually takes the form of food or a toy, and it is generally held in your hand so your dog can follow the scent with his nose. As he follows your hand movement he learns the hand signal that will subsequently be used to ask him to perform that particular skill. Lures are used frequently in the 21-Day Plan to teach the initial stages of a new skill, but once the hand signal has been learned, the lure is no longer necessary. Do not overuse lures; stop using them as soon as possible.

Developing complex behaviours

Teach each new activity in stages. Every time you and your dog practise (repeat) a skill, you need to mould the behaviour your dog is offering more closely into what you want as the final result. Perfecting the skill takes time and practice. The 21-Day Plan supports this approach by telling you

Assessment

which skills to repeat for reinforcement and when, and in this way builds on perfecting the skills. You will also find that the more advanced training towards the end of the plan uses a combination of skills learned earlier.

Commands

Your verbal and body signals are going to become cues for your dog to perform each behaviour. When you teach your dog to 'Sit', for example, the word you use and the body movement are both learned by your dog as meaning 'move into the sit position' – they function as a command.

Marking correct behaviour

Always let your dog know when he is in the correct position or performing in the way you ask.
● Mark desired behaviour simply by using a praise word such as 'Good Dog!' or 'Yes!' or using a clicker to make a click sound.
● Follow this marker with a valuable reward, so that your dog will remember that this is the exact thing he needs to do next time to earn that reward.
● Elderly or deaf dogs may respond better to a clear 'thumbs-up' hand signal.

● Every marker signal, whether a click, praise, or thumbs-up, must be followed by a reward.
● In the plan, praise is used as a marker and also a verbal reward.

Timing

Your timing of lure, command, marker, and reward need to be absolutely exact if your dog is to learn effectively. Given too soon, or too late, they will cease to have meaning for your dog.

Practise on people first!

Before starting the 21-Day Plan with your dog, hone your skills using family members as trainees.
● Practice luring them into a position (by standing on one leg or waving), mark the correct behaviour, and reward them.
● Do this without verbally explaining what you want them to do, since you will not be able to verbally explain to your dog, either.
● Make the command word something they will not already associate with that action, such as the word 'Red'.
　If you can teach them successfully, you can begin training your dog with the 21-Day Plan.

Part 2:
21-Day Training Plan

Your step-by-step guide to complete dog training

Before you start

By now you should have a clear assessment of your dog, and of your role as teacher. There are a few items you need to get together before starting the plan. The first thing is to create a training box or bag containing all the equipment you will need during training. This should include:

- Pen and notepaper.
- Collar, flat type. If your dog already has a collar, check that it fits correctly. It should be snug enough that you can only slide two fingers underneath it (one finger on a puppy or toy breed).
- A lead of approximately 1.2 m (4 ft), with a clip at the end to attach it to your dog's collar. Choose a lead that is comfortable to hold. Bridle leather leads are the most suitable for older dogs. Make sure the lead is not too heavy.
- A long line (approximately 10 m or 30 ft long), with a clip at the end. Polypropylene webbing is the best material for a long line, as it does not become overly heavy when wet, and it is light and comfortable to hold.
- Some house line (optional). This is a lightweight lead to use around the house; it needs to be around 0.5 m (2 ft) long, and made of webbing or nylon.
- Clicker (optional).
- Toys. Choose a selection of ragger-type toys, hollow chew toys (made of rubber) in which you can place food, balls on ropes, and perhaps one or two toys with squeakers inside.
- Food treats. Chop all your dog's food treats into small pieces, no larger than the size of your little fingernail. Use chicken, ham, cheese, or other strongly scented food that is suitable for your dog. You could look for a recipe for liver cake or other healthy treats online and make

them fresh to use as treats, rather than resorting to bought treats, which are rarely as effective as delicious-smelling fresh ones. Mix these tasty treats into a bag or plastic lidded pot along with a handful of your dog's normal kibble. This way, you reduce the risk of overfeeding him with rich, fattening foods. Measure out each day's portion of treats in advance to keep his weight stable. Make sure, too, that your family does not start handing out treats to your dog when he is in their company but not in the process of being trained.

Planning your days

You will find that some daily sessions require the help of other people or dogs, or an outdoor trip. Look through the plan in advance to see where you may need to recruit additional help. If this is difficult on a specific day, you can swap the days around a little, but it is better to make a point of sticking to the planned progression if at all possible. It may be a little inconvenient on some days, but you will benefit considerably if you maintain the plan whenever you can.

What to do if you miss a day

It is recommended that you keep to your planned pace (see pages 12–13), but if you do miss a day, simply pick up where you left off. You may need to repeat the previous day's training if the break is longer than a single day, to help remind your dog of the skills that he learned. Some dogs retain information better than others, so if he looks uncertain, go back to an easier stage until he is more confident.

The most important thing is to be consistent and have fun!

Day 1

Recognizing his name | Wearing a collar and lead | Recognizing his name | Wearing a collar and lead | SOCIALIZATION 1: New people New sounds

5 mins | 5 mins | REST | 5 mins | 10 mins | REST | 10 mins | 10 mins | REST & PLAY

Recognizing his name

Your dog's name offers a unique way to attract his attention. If you are renaming an older dog, it gives him a fresh start and a new, happy association. Never 'waste' your dog's name by repeatedly allowing him to ignore it. He needs to know that hearing his name means fun is on the way!

1 Sit a short distance from your dog, holding a treat or toy out of sight. Then bring it forward and begin to hold it out towards him. As he looks at you, say his name and immediately give him the treat or toy.

2 Hide the treat or toy out of sight again and wait for your dog to become distracted. Offer the treat or toy, and as he pays attention, say his name and again, reward with the treat or toy, then play with him. Repeat five times.

3 Wait for your dog to become distracted again and this time, say his name first. He should turn to you in anticipation. Offer the reward immediately and then play. Repeat three times.

Wearing a collar and lead

Dogs are not born wearing collars and leads, and puppies can find the sensation of wearing one overwhelming. An older dog may have formed an unpleasant association with it or be overcome with uncontrolled excitement. This exercise encourages calm behaviour.

1 Attach the collar while your dog is eating a tasty treat. Feed him several tidbits, then remove the collar. Repeat three times. Then, with his collar on, gently hold the collar with one hand and offer a treat with your other hand. Release the collar as he finishes the food. Repeat three times.

2 Sit near your dog (collar on) and offer him some food. Allow him to approach. As he takes the food and eats it, attach the lead. Avoid stepping towards him. If he becomes overexcited, step back and wait until he settles. Put the lead down to help calm him. Repeat four times.

3 Attach the lead to his collar and allow him to trail it around. Play with him and do other supervised activities to distract him. Occasionally, offer a treat and use the lead to draw him towards you. Repeat a few times, then remove the lead and put it away.

Socialization 1

You need to introduce your dog to daily sights and sounds in a fun way, so that he relaxes when hearing them and remains confident as they become a familiar part of his life. Dogs build trust through socialization exercises such as those given below.

New people, new sounds

Ask family members to spend time playing gently with your dog (supervise children carefully). Show them how to teach him his name and let them practise attaching his collar and lead. You need to introduce him to new sounds too; dogs have sensitive hearing, and home appliances can be deafening. Gradually introduce them by playing with your dog in an adjoining room while they are used. He will learn that noises may be loud, but are not threatening.

Day 2

5 mins	10 mins	REST	5 mins	10 mins	REST	10 mins	REST & PLAY

Recognizing his name (DAY 1)

Coming when called

Wearing a collar and lead (DAY 1)

Controlled play

HOUSETRAINING

Coming when called

Learning to respond to the command 'Come!' allows your dog more independence while giving you control over a great deal of his behaviour.

1 Show your dog that you are holding a tasty treat and then quickly move about 2 m (6 ft) away from him. Make your body language inviting by opening your arms wide. Crouch down if you can.

2 As he approaches you, say 'Come!' using an excited, high-pitched tone of voice. Hold the treat out in front of you so your dog walks towards your hand.

3 Lure your dog close to you using your treat hand so that you do not need to stretch out. Take his collar. Praise and release the treat once you have a firm hold. To earn the reward, he must learn to come close with your hand on his collar. Repeat ten times.

Controlled play

Play teaches dogs about how to interact physically. Show your dog how to play gently, so that he learns that play is about fun and self-control.

1 Choose a toy that is easy to take hold of even when it is in your dog's mouth. If your dog likes to grab and tug, choose a solid toy so that his teeth will not become hooked into it.

2 Hold the toy low to the ground and near your feet, to dissuade your dog from jumping up and snatching. Wiggle the toy while backing away from your dog, to encourage him to follow it.

3 Allow him to chase the toy briefly, then stop moving it, so that it is less interesting. If he lets go, praise him. Have treats ready to swap for the toy if necessary. Repeat five times, then put the toy away.

Housetraining

You will need to remind your dog of the route to his toileting area. This consolidates his initial learning and will makes sure that a new puppy or rescue dog forms a good, lifelong habit.

Decide which part of the garden your dog should use for toileting and which exit door he should use. Place treats in a lidded container and hang it up or place it on a high shelf near the chosen door so your dog can see the container but not reach it. When you know he is ready to toilet (after eating, drinking, playing, waking, or training), encourage him to follow you along the route to the toilet area. Attach his lead so that you can keep him close to your chosen place in case he wanders too far. As soon as he toilets, say 'Hurry up!', then offer praise and a treat from your reward container. He will quickly learn to focus on following this route when he needs to toilet.

Day 3

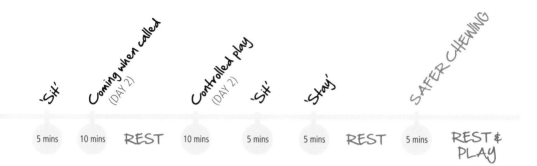

'Sit' — 5 mins

Coming when called (DAY 2) — 10 mins

REST

Controlled play (DAY 2) — 10 mins

'Sit' — 5 mins

'Stay' — 5 mins

REST

SAFER CHEWING — 5 mins

REST & PLAY

'Sit'

Learning to respond correctly to the 'Sit' command is a modest achievement but fundamental to all good dog behaviour.

1. Hold a treat close to your dog's nose and allow him to sniff it. You should be able to get him to follow your hand using this lure. Keeping the lure hand close to his nose, move it slowly towards the top of his head so that he looks up.

2. Continue moving your hand upwards until he starts to sit in an effort to reach the food. As he sits, say 'Sit', and offer praise and a treat. Repeat Steps 1 and 2 four times.

3. Then begin to say 'Sit' just before he sits (repeat five times). Finally, repeat with an empty hand, using the same hand signal and verbal command. Reward him. Repeat Step 3 from a standing position.

'Stay'

The 'Sit' command is only really useful if you can persuade your dog to stay seated! This command will keep your dog safely rooted.

1 Ask your dog to 'Sit' and keep his attention on your raised hand signal. Count to two and reward his patience. Then give your dog a release command: 'Go play!'.

2 Repeat, but take one pace away from your dog while maintaining focus on the hand signal. Immediately return to your dog, reward, and give the release command.

3 Ask him to sit, then move three paces away before returning. Gradually increase the time away from him. At times, drop back to a simple one-second sit to maintain his enthusiasm.

Safer chewing

A puppy chews to explore and play, and when he is teething, while older dogs find chewing to be a calming and enjoyable activity. However, you will need to direct your dog's chewing onto suitable items such as hollow rubber toys, by using a scrape of cheese or meat spread inside. Don't allow him to destroy items – even dog toys contain squeakers and fillings that can harm if ingested. Prevent access to valuable possessions: your dog cannot distinguish costly items from ordinary ones! If your dog chews something you do not want him to have, calmly redirect his attention to a tastier option. Always swap. If he steals items to chew, or grabs at clothing or hands, use a lead on his collar to control him. This prevents chasing games developing. Tired puppies like to chew gently on something ('mouthing'), so offer him the chance to rest in his bed with a chew to occupy him.

Day 4

'Down'

'Sit' and 'Stay' (DAY 3)

Coming when called (DAY 2)

FREE CHOICE

Learning to be left alone

| 5 mins | 5 mins | REST | 5 mins | 10 mins | REST | 5 mins | REST & PLAY |

'Down'

Like the 'Sit' command, the 'Down' command is a fundamental skill. It provides the foundation for many other commands, and will prove invaluable for times when you need your dog to wait quietly for you, while you visit a shop, for instance.

1 Sit or kneel near your dog. Hold a treat in your hand and allow him to sniff this lure. You may prefer to begin with your dog in a 'Sit' position at first, as it means his back legs will already be in the correct position for the 'Down' command.

2 Lower your hand slowly, aiming for the gap on the floor between your dog's front paws. His body will begin to crouch and lower to the floor. Move your hand slowly to the floor between his paws and towards his body.

3 Once his chest touches the floor, say 'Down', then praise and release the treat. Repeat four times, gradually increasing the pace until your hand dropping becomes the hand signal for 'Down'. Repeat with no treat in your hand.

Free choice

Every now and then you need to conduct a training session that reflects your dog's individual needs. For instance, your dog may need additional practice on a task he found more difficult, or that you feel he did not quite master. On the other hand, a young or elderly dog may simply need a break, in which case you can use this session to calmly interact with your dog. Make sure you plan to do something, even if you just make notes about your levels of achievement so far.

Pacing review

Is your 21-Day Plan going at the pace you anticipated, or have you set your expectations too high? If you feel the pace is too slow, offer your dog additional practice sessions, but don't jump ahead of the day-to-day plan. This could burn out the enthusiasm that must be maintained for long-term success.

Learning to be left alone

Your dog must learn that being alone for short periods is enjoyable in a safe haven. A crate is not essential, but it does prevent damage, aid housetraining, and reduce attention-seeking activities. Some dogs take longer to adjust, so don't worry if he is reluctant.

1 Prepare a suitable den such as a crate or quiet corner. Place a comfy bed inside with water in a non-spill bowl. Cover the top of the crate with a lightweight sheet or towel (caution: this may get chewed).

2 Place a tasty chew toy in the den. If your dog is reluctant to enter, throw additional food treats into the den. Say 'Den' as he enters and praise. Allow him to leave freely as he chooses. Repeat five times.

3 While your dog is occupied in the den, walk a few paces away, then return. Repeat a few times, then call your dog from the den. Practise this several times each day.

Day 5

Food manners   Down' and 'Stay' (DAY 4) AND (DAY 3)   Walking on a loose lead   SOCIALIZATION 2: Getting used to traffic   Meeting children   Learning to be left alone (DAY 4)

5 mins   10 mins   REST   10 mins   REST   10 mins   10 mins   REST   5 mins   REST & PLAY

Food manners

Your dog must learn that just because food is in your hand, it is not intended for him unless invited.

1. From a sitting position, hold some treats in your hand. Keep your hand open at first. Stay quiet and relaxed, and do not make direct eye contact with him.

2. As your dog sniffs at your hand, close it into a fist so that he cannot reach the food. Keep your hand still and stay calm and quiet. If he nibbles at your hand, wear a glove at first.

3. As your dog gives up and moves back, immediately open your hand and offer the treat to him. As he moves up to your hand again, close it immediately. Repeat several times until he confidently sits back, ignores the food hand, and waits for his reward instead.

Socialization 2

Getting used to traffic

It's important for your dog to stay calm around traffic, so gradually introduce him to the noises, smells, and movement of vehicles. Visit a moderately busy road for a few minutes, stroking him all the time and offering tasty food each time a vehicle passes. If he refuses to eat, retreat a little until he becomes calmer, and move closer gradually. Once he is confident, add in some 'Sit' training.

Meeting children

Invite friends with children to come with you on a walk. Ask them to stand further along the path so that your dog 'meets' them. Allow him to sniff them if he chooses, but ask the children not to reach out to him at first. Offer him treats to increase his enjoyment.

Walking on a loose lead

Dogs need to learn that a tight lead does not take them they way they want to go. Remember – it takes two to pull on a lead!

Discourage pulling

Stand still with your dog on a lead. As he moves forward, before the lead tightens, take a pace or two back and gently steer him back to your side. Once he waits calmly (this make take a few tries, but be patient), walk with him in the direction he wanted to explore. This gives him his reward without pulling.

Teach him to follow

In an enclosed space, run away from your off-lead dog, encouraging him to follow. As he reaches you, change direction. Keep changing direction so that he stays attentive. Slow down if he becomes overexcited. He will soon match your pace perfectly, without racing ahead.

Day 6

'Stand'

'Down' and 'Stay'
(DAY 4) AND (DAY 3)

'Off' and Take it'

Walking on a loose lead
(DAY 5)

HIDE AND SEEK

| 5 mins | 5 mins | REST | 5 mins | 10 mins | REST | 10 mins | REST & PLAY |

'Stand'

Teaching a confident 'Stand' allows you and other people to examine your dog and groom him calmly.

1 Begin with your dog in a 'Sit' or 'Down' position. Hold a treat on his nose and then move it towards you and away from him, using a sideways hand motion, at the same time raising it slightly so that he moves into the 'Stand' position.

2 Move your hand slightly back towards his nose again to stop him stepping forward. Keep your hand in that position and say 'Stand', then praise and give him the treat. Repeat five times.

3 Keep your hand in the same position, but start to move slightly away from him; he should remain standing but not follow you. The sideways motion becomes the 'Stand' hand signal.

'Off' and 'Take it'

'Off' is used to stop dogs jumping up at people, lunging, or stealing items. 'Take it' gives your dog the cue that he can accept the reward.

1 Offer your dog a tasty treat. If food manners training was successful, he should sniff and then sit back. As he does so, say 'Off' and praise him.

2 Pass the treat to him and say 'Take it'. Do not allow him to come forward to take the treat – you must give it to him. Gradually expect him to stay further away as you say 'Off' by giving the command before he sniffs the treat. Only reward when he stays further back.

3 Always go towards your dog to reward him following the 'Off' command. He will learn to wait patiently at a distance for the reward to come to him on the cue 'Take it', rather than jumping up to get it. Repeat this exercise with a visitor that your dog knows.

Hide and seek

This game allows you to build a strong recall bond as your dog learns to look for you. While your dog is in the room, move excitedly away and partially hide yourself behind a piece of furniture. Make it easy for him to spot you. Call him happily and praise him as he finds you. Next, hide somewhere a little harder to locate, but still praise success. If he is uncertain, show him that you are holding a treat or toy before you hide. Practise a few times, then ask someone to hold his collar, or practise his 'Stay', while you hide further away.

Hiding outdoors
Take someone with you on walks so that they can hold the lead while you run and hide behind trees in the park, for example. Alternatively, use a long line to give your dog more freedom to hunt and sniff for you!

Day 7

'Watch me'   'Stand' (DAY 6)   'Off' and Take it' (DAY 6)   Walking to heel   SOCIALIZATION 3: Visitor party   Circle game

5 mins   5 mins   5 mins   REST   10 mins   REST   10 mins   10 mins   REST & PLAY

'Watch me'

This command means that you can pull your dog's attention away from another potentially distracting event or person, and focus on you. It is an essential command to learn, because unless you have your dog's attention, you will be unable to ask him to do anything.

1 Squat down near your dog and softly call his name. As he turns towards you, say his name again and raise your hand to eye level as you do so. The goal is to get him to lift his head and follow the movement of your hand, without jumping up.

2 As he follows your hand movement and makes eye contact with you, say 'Watch me'. Praise and treat. Repeat three times until he is making confident eye contact for several seconds. Release each time while saying 'Go play'.

3 Repeat Steps 1 and 2 with your dog to the side of you instead of in front of you, so that his head turns towards you on 'Watch me'. Repeat on both sides of your body to indicate to your dog that eye contact and head turn is your goal.

Walking to heel

Train your dog to stay close at heel when walking past distractions or on narrow pathways. Heel should be considered a 'moving Stay' position.

1 Position your dog, on a lead, beside you, near your feet. Hold a treat or toy in the hand nearest to him as a lure. Step forward a single pace and pat your leg to encourage him to follow. Say 'Heel' as he moves next to you, praise, and reward. Repeat five times.

2 Walk two or three steps with your dog at heel, stopping and rewarding each time. If he is not in the correct position, the lead will start to tighten. If this happens, stop and reposition him back in the heel position, then start again from the beginning.

3 As he walks in the heel position, say 'Heel' repeatedly, while also praising and rewarding him. Repeat several times, then rest and play.

Socialization 3

Visitor party

Invite some friends to your home for a 'socialization party'. Allow them to play with your dog, using toys and treats, but supervise for any signs of uncertainty. Distract your dog regularly and offer him a break, giving him the chance to return later if he wishes. If this goes well, ask visitors to put on hats, sunglasses, or some kind of fancy dress and then play with him. Keep treats and toys frequent. Allow your dog to go over and sniff each person and retreat as he chooses.

Circle game

Ask visitors to sit in a circle, and give each person two treats. One person in the circle calls your dog over to them, asks him to sit, then gives him the treat. They nominate another person in the circle to do the same. Repeat until everyone has had two turns.

Day 8

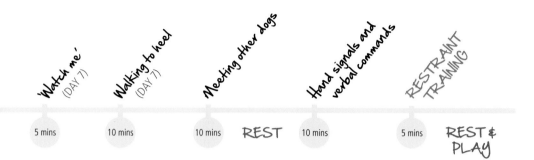

Watch me' (DAY 7) — 5 mins

Walking to heel (DAY 7) — 10 mins

Meeting other dogs — 10 mins

REST

Hand signals and verbal commands — 10 mins

RESTRAINT TRAINING — 5 mins

REST & PLAY

Meeting other dogs

It is extremely important for your dog to learn how to greet other dogs calmly, and only when you allow it. This skill is easily taught, but you will need to enlist the help of a fellow dog-owner.

1 Team up with an owner and dog you know to be confident and calm. Ask them to remain in place while you approach them from 20 paces away. As soon as your dog shows interest in them, step back, call him away and reward.

2 Repeat several times, each time allowing him to get closer to the other dog, before stepping back, calling him away and rewarding him each time. If he stays calm, finally reward him by allowing the dogs to briefly sniff one another for a few seconds.

3 Happily call your dog away from the other dog, offering a treat or toy. Gently guide him with his lead if he is reluctant. Once he returns to you, allow him to go back to the other dog for a longer greeting, then go for a walk together with your new friends.

Hand signals and verbal commands

Which does your dog notice more – hand signals or spoken commands?
Make a review of the cues you are offering to make sure your training
stays on track and that you are delivering clear messages to your dog.

Hand signals

A hand is lifted for 'Sit', moves
downwards for 'Down', sideways
for 'Stand', and stays in place for
'Stay'. For 'Watch me', your hand
lifts to your eyes. In each case,
hold a small piece of food in the
signal hand. Practise each one
to check that your dog clearly
understands them. Say each
command aloud only once.

Verbal commands

Are you repeating verbal
commands often? This may
be because you think your
dog has not heard, but you
need to resist the temptation.
Repeating verbal cues reduces
their effectiveness. As dogs are
masters at observing our bodies
(including hand signals), verbal
nagging has little effect.

Happy to be held

In addition to 'Stand' (Day 6),
you will need to hold your dog
steady for treatment at the vet
and for grooming. This gentle
restraint should be welcome,
not frightening. It allows you to
physically move or steer your
dog in times of emergency. See
'Restraint training' below for
extra tips.

Restraint training

Gently hold your dog's collar and place a toy or treat on
the floor just out of reach. As he pulls forward to claim
it, gently prevent him for a few seconds, offering him
small tidbits. As he calms, pick up the 'temptation' and
give it to him. If he struggles, use a less-tempting treat
or toy, until he happily accepts that waiting and being
held is enjoyable.

Repeat this exercise with increasingly tempting
targets until he has learned that being held back is still
rewarding. Ask family members and friends to practise
this with him too, so that he becomes accustomed to
restraint from others.

Day 9

Meeting other dogs (DAY 8)   RESTRAINT TRAINING (DAY 8)   'Roll over'   'Go to bed'   SOCIALIZATION 4: Ready for teeth cleaning   Calm to the touch

10 mins   5 mins   REST   10 mins   10 mins   REST   5 mins   5 mins

'Roll over'

This gives your dog confidence to roll onto his back without feeling vulnerable and is ideal for examining his tummy or to trim claws.

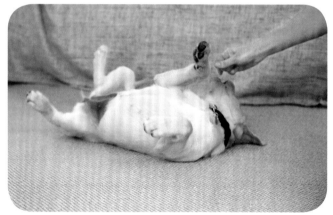

1 Get your dog into a 'Down' position. Place a treat by his nose and start to move the treat to his side, to lure his head sideways. Keep the treat close to his body so that he looks over his shoulder. Continue the hand movement until his whole body rolls onto its side.

2 Once he is on his side, reward and release. Repeat three times. Next, while he is lying on his side, continue to move your hand slowly so that he rolls onto his back then over to his other side, as his head follows your hand.

3 Once he has completed the full rotation, say 'Roll over', then praise and reward. Repeat, then rest. From time to time, give your dog an enjoyable tummy rub or examine his paws, always giving him a treat to finish.

'Go to bed'

This command gives your dog a specific target to run to should you need him to move from elsewhere in the home or to settle for a nap.

1 Stand near your dog's bed, holding a toy or treat. Throw the reward to the bed and as your dog jumps onto the bed to reach it, say 'Bed'. Repeat three times, then take a few paces away and repeat three more times.

2 Stand further away from his bed. Move your arm in the same throwing gesture as you say 'Bed' but do not release the reward on to the bed. Wait for your dog to move to the bed, and only then throw and praise. Repeat three times.

3 Gradually increase the distance you stand from the bed until you can send your dog there from all angles using this command and arm gesture. Once he is on the bed, command him to 'Stay' (repeat Day 3's 'Stay' training in this new location).

Socialization 4

Ready for teeth cleaning

Use tasty toothpaste designed for dogs, which he will enjoy licking from your finger or dog toothbrush. Allow him to do this, then move away. As he comes back for more, touch his mouth gently with your other hand. Briefly begin lifting his lip to expose his teeth. Repeat, then rest. Give him the opportunity to move away whenever he chooses. If he moves away, there is no tasty toothpaste reward for him. If he stays, increase touching until you are able to open his mouth a little wider each time. Keep sessions short.

Calm to the touch

People, particularly children, reach down to dogs from above, bending over them to show affection. Teach your dog to welcome these gestures. Several times a day, ask your dog to sit, then bend your body forward, offering a treat or toy if he stays settled.

Day 10

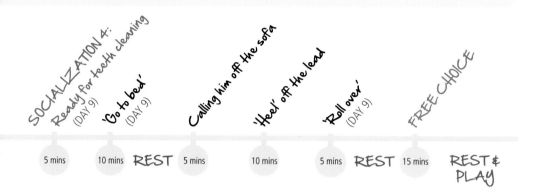

SOCIALIZATION 4:
Ready for teeth cleaning
(DAY 9)

'Go to bed'
(DAY 9)

Calling him off the sofa

'Heel' off the lead

'Roll over'
(DAY 9)

FREE CHOICE

| 5 mins | 10 mins | REST | 5 mins | 10 mins | 5 mins | REST | 15 mins | REST & PLAY |

Calling him off the sofa

Sofas are comfortable – they are raised away from draughts and warmed by you. Of course your dog likes to lie there! It is a matter of personal choice whether or not he is allowed to, but do teach him to move on or off so he only jumps on the sofa when you have given him permission.

1 Encourage your dog to get onto the sofa. He will learn that he may only get up when invited. Then step back and call him off the sofa to you ('Come'), using a toy or treat to encourage him.

2 As he moves off the sofa, praise enthusiastically. If he does not move towards you, do not challenge him or reach for him. Next time you practise, attach a lead to his collar so that you can calmly draw him to you. Always reward well.

3 Use the 'Off' command (Day 6, page 35) to prevent your dog from getting up onto the sofa in the first place. Call him to you, and even if he looks at the sofa, offer him praise, then send him to his nearby bed instead.

Free choice

Distraction work

By now you have quite a repertoire of training commands and signals, but your dog needs to perform them everywhere. For this free-choice session, pick a task and practise it in a busy place. If your dog appears unsure, make the task very easy. If it is still tricky, re-visit the chart at the end of this book (pages 92–93) to make certain your dog does not lack socialization in this area.

Reducing the food or toy lure

Using an exercise in which your dog is confident, fade out the use of the food or toy so that you are not holding it in your hand for the training. This is something that you will need to do with all exercises in future.

'Heel' off the lead

This skill allows you to build up your confidence at walking with your dog off the lead. Your dog will learn to walk next to you freely, but under control. Gradually build up distractions around you as you walk, so that he learns to ignore them and stay with you.

1 In an enclosed area, attach the lead to your dog's collar and hold it lightly. Call your dog to the heel position (see Day 7, page 37), and walk a few paces – as you do so, allow the lead to trail on the ground. Praise and give the release command.

2 Call your dog to heel again, allow the lead to trail, but walk 10 paces before giving the release command. Do this five times, increasing by two paces each time (as long as he is always attentive) until you reach 20 paces. Finish and play.

3 Finally, remove his lead and repeat from Step 1 of this exercise. Practise until you are confident that your dog will remain attentive whether or not his lead is attached. Then practise in busier locations, attaching a long line if you are uncertain at first. Keep rewards visible and frequent.

Day 11

Calling him off the sofa (DAY 10)

Heel (DAY 10)

'Give a paw'

Getting into and out of the car

LONG-LINE TRAINING

10 mins   10 mins   REST   5 mins   10 mins   REST   10 mins   REST & PLAY

'Give a paw'

This is perfect for claw clipping and a lovely greeting too. It helps teach older dogs not to scratch, as it permits only paw-to-hand contact.

1. Ask your dog to 'Sit'. Then hold a treat in one hand and use your other hand to lift one of his front paws a very short distance from the ground. Say 'Paw', then praise and reward before releasing. Repeat five times. Be careful not to unbalance your dog.

2. Once your dog accepts having his paw lifted, as you begin to say 'Paw', drop your hand to his foot and wait. He should anticipate and begin to lift his foot in readiness. Praise this movement when you see it, and immediately reward. Repeat four times.

3. This time, when your dog lifts his paw, gradually raise your hand a little so that he stretches his paw to place it in the palm of your flattened hand. Hold his paw for a few seconds, praise and release. Repeat four times.

Getting into and out of the car

Safety and steadiness when entering and leaving a car is essential. A young or elderly dog may need you to lift him in and out.

1. Place your dog in a car while it is parked on a driveway. Tell him to 'Sit'. Open the door a crack. If he moves, close the door – but be careful not to trap him in the closing door.

2. Once your dog is steady, open the door more fully and call or lift him from the car. Repeat this exercise in reverse, asking him to stay sitting calmly while you open the door.

3. Once he sits calmly while you open and shut the car door, invite him to get into the car and 'Sit' to finish. If he is reluctant, throw some treats into the car first.

Long-line training

To improve confidence before letting your dog completely off the lead, you could try attaching a long line to his collar. Caution: do not entangle anyone's legs or objects in the line.

For recall and to prevent chasing

In a quiet location, attach the long line and hold it halfway along its length. Allow your dog to roam and sniff for a few minutes, then call him back to you for a reward. If he is reluctant or sees something to chase, gather up the long line and draw him back to you gently. For off-lead walking at heel, attach the long line and command your dog to heel. Walk a few paces, then calmly tell him 'Go play'. Allow him time for a brief sniff, then call him back to heel. Repeat three times, then play.

Day 12

Getting into and out of the car (DAY 11)   'Give paw' (DAY 11)   CHASE ME!   LONG-LINE TRAINING (DAY 11)   Examining ears and eyes   Sit before food bowl

10 mins   5 mins   REST   10 mins   10 mins   REST   10 mins   5 mins   REST & PLAY

Sit before food bowl

Mealtimes are a great training opportunity, allowing you to teach your dog to be a little more patient when faced with his dinner.

1 Allow your dog to watch you preparing his food, then stand in readiness with the bowl in your hand. Tell your dog to 'Sit' and 'Stay'. Wait patiently until he does so, and do not repeat your commands.

2 Once he is settled, begin to lower the food bowl to the ground. If he shifts position, straighten up and wait for him to sit again. Start lowering the bowl once more.

3 Your dog must sit and wait while the bowl is placed on the ground. He should soon realize that staying still means that dinner will be given more quickly. Once the bowl is placed, release your dog to eat.

Examining ears and eyes

Examine your dog's ears and eyes regularly to check for any problems, and teach him that this is just as enjoyable as being petted. Your dog will feel more confident if you have practised doing this with him before he has to undergo a vet's examination.

Examining eyes

Follow the instructions for examining ears (see left), but check your dog's eyes instead. Eye problems need prompt medical attention, so contact your vet immediately if you suspect there is a problem.

Examining ears

Ask your dog to 'Sit', and stroke his head calmly. Now and again, touch his ears while talking softly to him, lifting them gently. If he stays relaxed, look a little closer into each ear. Reward with a treat. Repeat with the other ear. Allow him to move away if he chooses, but provide extra tasty treats to attract him to stay.

Chase me!

This is a high-energy game that helps to improve recall for all ages of dog. Pace the game so that your dog does not become over-excited or try to nip.

1 In an enclosed area, let your dog off the lead. Walk forward, placing a toy ahead of your dog, then suddenly turn away and run past your dog, calling him excitedly so that he chases after you and not the toy on the ground. When he reaches you, play excitedly with another toy.

2 Collect the first toy, and repeat Step 1 three times, then start to throw, rather than place, the first toy. If your dog finds this difficult, go back to dropping the first toy onto the ground. Always dash away excitedly, even if your dog makes a mistake, and reward him well when he comes to you.

Day 13

Examining ears and eyes (DAY 12)   5 mins

Chase me! (DAY 12)   5 mins

REST

Ssh… stop barking!   5 mins

Meeting people politely   15 mins

REST

TOYS FOR BRAIN GAMES   10 mins

REST & PLAY

Ssh… stop barking!

This exercise is aimed to deal with excitement barking, rather than barking due to fear or stress (see pages 68–69 and 89 for information and tips on managing other barking problems).

1 Arrange for a family member to come to your front door, or just to make a knocking sound, if this usually causes your dog to bark. Have some strongly scented treats in your hand. As he barks, hold a treat directly on his nose.

2 As he stops barking to sniff the treat, say 'Ssh' and hold a finger to your lips with your other hand. Count to five while he stays quiet, then praise and release the treat. Only give praise and a treat after a period of silence.

3 Repeat Steps 1 and 2 until your dog simply looks at you quietly when he hears the knock. If you prefer, allow one or two barks only, before giving the command. Only reward your dog after he has stayed quiet after hearing knocks. Otherwise he will learn to bark to gain a reward.

Meeting people politely

It is very important for your dog to learn how to greet people calmly and politely, whether he knows them or not.

1 Arrange for some friends to meet you at separate locations along your normal walk route. Take your dog out for a walk, and as soon as you spot a friend walking towards you, ask your dog to 'Sit' and 'Stay'.

2 If your dog is very excited, ask the person to wait at a short distance without making eye contact with your dog, until your dog becomes calmer. Then allow him or her to get closer.

3 Allow your friend and your dog to say a brief hello, then call your dog to heel and walk past your friend. If your dog finds this difficult, be patient, as it may take several tries before he learns that people only say 'hello' to a calm dog.

Toys for brain games

For independent stimulation, choose toys that engage your dog's prey drive. No matter what his life stage, his sense of smell will engage this instinct and bring it into play.

● Place your dog's dinner inside treat balls, cubes, or hollow rubber toys. Or place food inside a sealed cardboard box for him to tear into. Teach your dog to 'forage' by helping him find the food at first. Chopped-up carrot or apple are low-calorie fillings.

● Complex toys require an interactive approach. Choose a puzzle toy that requires a learned skill, such as lifting out a puzzle piece or sliding a cover to reach food inside a box. Help your dog to work it out at first and don't let him chew on the toy. With guidance he will find this a calm but stimulating activity.

Day 14

Meeting people politely
(DAY 13)

Ssh... stop barking!
(DAY 13)

Come to heel

Find it!'

TOUCHING A TARGET

10 mins   10 mins   REST   10 mins   10 mins   REST   10 mins   REST & PLAY

Come to heel

Use this to direct your dog to the heel position from any angle or distance. This can be handy even inside the home, if you want to call your dog to stand close beside you for any reason.

1 Stand with your dog in front of you. Place a treat on his nose, then step back with your left leg. As you do so, lure your dog towards your left side by swinging back your left hand (holding the treat).

2 Move your hand slightly away from your leg to swing your dog slightly outwards. Start to circle your hand back to your side in an anti-clockwise direction.

3 Step your left leg forwards again so that your dog turns into the heel position as you move forward. Say 'Heel' and praise him well, giving him the treat. Repeat with your dog in different starting positions.

'Find it!'

Let your dog show you how well he can use his sense of smell to locate hidden items by using this simple technique.

1 Show your dog one of his favourite toys, or use a treat inside a lidded pot. In full view of your dog, place this item underneath a cushion or blanket.

2 Encourage your dog to look for the item and as he does so, say 'Find it!'. Praise him well as soon as he locates the item and reward him with the toy or treat. Repeat several times, then hide the item in the same place but don't let your dog see you placing it.

3 Extend this training by hiding the item in a different place on each of the next three repetitions, then rest. Once he is confident, choose hiding places that are increasingly difficult to locate, such as in the garden or among long grass on your walk.

Touching a target

You can teach your dog to touch a marker, which can then be used to train him on to more advanced behaviours, such as closing doors or pressing a lever. First you need to create a simple target – this can be a circle of card or a plastic lid. If you like, attach some ribbon to it, so that you can hang the target wherever you choose.

Nose push
Start by placing the target on the ground. Place a treat at its centre. As your dog goes to eat the treat, say 'Touch' and praise him. It will take around four to six repetitions before your dog will start to run confidently to the marker. Begin to say 'Touch' just as he starts to move, so he learns to seek the target on command. Repeat five times. Then remove the treat from the target and repeat the exercise. Be patient and your dog will still run to the target. As he lowers his nose to sniff, praise and throw the treat. Repeat five times.

Day 15

Come to heel (DAY 14)   Find it! (DAY 14)   Settle down   Doorway control   SOCIALIZATION 5: Visiting the vet or pet shop   Visiting a café

| 5 mins | 5 mins | REST | 10 mins | 10 mins | REST | 10 mins | 10 mins | REST & PLAY |

Settle down

Teaching your dog self-control – by knowing how to settle down – is simple if you incorporate the excitement of a game with frequent settling-down periods.

1 Play with your dog using a toy, keeping the game reasonably calm. Use a rubber or plastic toy that he cannot easily tug.

2 After a couple of minutes, stop playing. Produce a small treat and swap this for the toy, telling your dog 'Down!'. When he lies down, praise him, count to three, then say 'Go play!' and start playing with the toy again.

3 Repeat these stages four to six times, adding on an extra second to the 'Down' count each time. The reward for settling down becomes the game with the toy, teaching your dog to switch off excitement without frustration.

Socialization 5

Visiting the vet or pet shop

Your dog needs to experience and enjoy visits to the vet long before an emergency arises, so ask your surgery if there are times that you can call in with him, even if only for a quick hello and a treat. Pet shops often welcome dogs, so on another day, ask your local pet shop if you can visit. Take your dog to choose a new toy or to buy a small treat. Allow him to greet the staff in his own time, and use the opportunity to practise your training skills.

Visiting a café

Find a café where dogs are permitted. Take a small mat or towel for him to lie on. If people want to stroke him, ask them to offer him a treat first, or offer him one yourself. Only allow interaction if he is keen.

Doorway control

For safety reasons, your dog must learn that he must not go through a door unless specifically invited. This protects him and prevents him chasing into the road or jumping up at callers.

1 With your dog on a lead, stand near a door, positioning your dog a lead's length away from the door itself. As you reach for the door, he may move to reach it. Calmly reposition him back to his starting point, using his lead.

2 Repeat until you can reach for the door without his attempting to move. Next, open the door a crack. If he rushes forwards, close the door, taking care not to trap him. Gently move him back to his original spot.

3 Repeat until you can open the door widely while he remains in place. Only release him to walk through the door when you have already stepped through yourself. This allows you to check it is safe before you call him through.

Day 16

Doorway control
(DAY 15)

Settle down
(DAY 15)

FREE CHOICE

'Come away'

Peep through legs

10 mins   5 mins   REST   15 mins   REST   10 mins   10 mins   REST & PLAY

'Come away'

Teach your dog to actively turn away from something he wants and to come straight back to you instead. He must learn to do this whenever you say 'Come away', even from cats, other dogs, or dropped food.

1 Ask your dog to sit, and place a favourite toy directly in front of him. He must remain sitting whilst you do so. If he dashes forward, remove the toy and try again. Hold a second toy or treat in your hand.

2 Sit behind your dog and call him to you. As he turns away from the toy to face you, say 'Come away' and back away a little to encourage him to come close. Praise him and reward.

3 If your dog is reluctant to turn away from the toy, use a lead to draw him gently away. Each time he turns away, praise him well. Never let him return to the toy on the ground as this gives an inconsistent message. 'Come away' means leave, never to return!

Peep through legs

This is a fun trick that will give your dog confidence at moving and settling close to you without touching your legs at all.

1 Begin with your dog in a 'Sit' behind you. Standing in front of him, place your legs slightly more than hip-width apart, so they form a 'V' shape. Hold a treat or toy lure in one hand.

2 Reach through the gap in the 'V' with your lure, and waggle it so that your dog comes towards it and follows it as you draw it through the gap. His head will come through the gap. Stop just before your dog's front feet pass your own.

3 Ask your dog to sit or stand in place, then praise and reward. Repeat three times with your dog starting from further behind you. Then practise from Step 1 again but with your dog starting first to your side and then from in front of you.

Free choice

Explore a new place

For your free choice session today, why not take your dog for a walk in a brand new location? Pick somewhere you have not visited before, such as local woods or a shopping street, where you can practise any of the previous days' sessions. He may also get the opportunity to meet new canine and human friends to help continue his socialization.

Relaxation and massage

Take time to have a relaxing session with your dog, gently stroking him. Notice which areas of the body he enjoys having massaged and get to know what kind of touch helps him to settle. You can use this knowledge when praising your dog or calming him.

Day 17

'Come away' (DAY 16)	Peep through legs (DAY 16)		'Fetch!'	'Spin!'		CLOSE THE DOOR	
15 mins	5 mins	REST	10 mins	5 mins	REST	10 mins	REST & PLAY

'Fetch!'

This command teaches your dog that toys must always be returned to you if he wants another game. It provides great exercise, too. By using a corner, you can discourage him from running away with the toy.

1 Start by sitting on the floor or in a chair, pointing towards a corner of the room with your left hand. In your right hand, start moving around a soft toy such as a ragger, keeping it close to the ground. As your dog starts to follow it, toss it into the corner.

2 Encourage your dog to pick up the toy. He will need to turn back to you as the corner prevents him running away with it. As he does so, praise him excitedly!

3 Play with the toy again a little more excitedly, then repeat from Step 1. If your dog is reluctant to release the toy, swap it for a treat before continuing. Repeat three times, then put the toy away.

Close the door

Using 'nose push' target training from Day 14 (see page 51), you can teach your dog to close the door, by placing the target about a third of the way up the door panel. Any door, even a low kitchen cupboard, is suitable.

Start by attaching the target to an open door. Hold a treat near the centre of the target and give the 'Touch' command. As he touches the target, praise well and release the treat. Repeat four times; on the fifth time, withhold the treat and ask him to 'Touch' again. He must push the target a little harder this time before you praise and treat. Praise and treat the strongest pushes until the door actually moves. Once he is confidently pushing the door, remove the target and just say 'Touch!'. With practice, he will be able to push the door until it closes.

'Spin!'

Fun and exciting, a spin can be added to your repertoire of tricks to show everyone how much fun you are both having on this 21-day programme!

1 With your dog in front of you, hold a treat or toy lure in one hand. As he follows it with his head, begin to turn your hand in a circular motion over his head.

2 Once his head has turned, continue the circular movement. Waggle your hand to keep his interest in the lure and as he is turning, say 'Spin!'.

3 As he completes the turn, praise him well and give him the treat or a game with the toy. Repeat once more, then rest. You do not want him to feel dizzy!

Day 18

CLOSE THE DOOR (DAY 17)

'Spin!' (DAY 17)

'Fetch!' (DAY 17)

'Give'

LEAVING OTHER DOGS

'Hold'

| 15 mins | 5 mins | 10 mins | REST | 5 mins | 5 mins | REST | 10 mins |

'Give'

Teach your dog that giving up an item to you always means he will be rewarded, rather than challenged. As he is learning this, encourage him to drop the item into your hand if possible.

1 Give your dog one of his favourite toys. While he is holding this, pick up another toy or a treat and hold it a short distance away from one side of his head, so that he can only reach it by turning.

2 Waggle the treat or toy, and as your dog turns towards it, offer it to him so that he drops the toy he is holding. As he does so, say 'Give', then praise him and let him have the treat or toy you are holding.

3 Repeat Steps 1 and 2 several times, making this into a give-and-take game. When your dog swaps the toy readily on 'Give', place your hand underneath the toy you want him to drop. Praise him well as it lands in your hand.

Leaving other dogs

Work on your dog's recall skills so that you can always call him away, no matter how actively he is playing with other dogs. Choose a walk in a busy location such as a park. If the environment is secure, your dog can be off-lead, but if you are uncertain, keep him on a lead. As soon as your dog notices another dog, take a pace back quickly and say 'Come away', praising him excitedly when he comes to you. Then allow him to play with the other dog as a reward. Practise calling him away again, then allowing him to continue play. If he is reluctant, use his lead to gently draw him away.

'Hold'

Asking your dog to hold and carry objects for you is a great way to encourage a helpful bond. This command and skill is slightly different to 'Fetch', as the object is not thrown first.

2 Encourage him to reach forward to take the toy. As his mouth closes around the toy, praise him and say 'Hold'. Encourage him to hold it for a few seconds, then say 'Give'. Repeat three times, then rest.

3 If your dog tries to snatch at the toy, calmly hold it still and ask him to 'Sit' and 'Stay' before commencing. Some dogs may not be keen to hold a toy at all; if this is the case, use a chew stick or hide food inside a hollow toy to motivate your dog.

1 Crouch down and ask your dog to sit on the floor in front of you. Hold either end of a toy that is easy for him to grip with his mouth. Choose a toy that you know he enjoys playing with.

Day 19

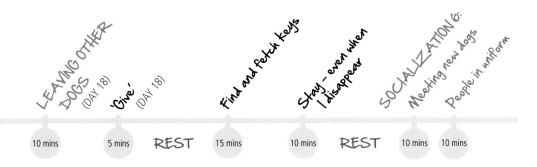

LEAVING OTHER DOGS (DAY 18) | 'Give' (DAY 18) | Find and fetch keys | Stay – even when I disappear | SOCIALIZATION 6: Meeting new dogs | People in uniform

10 mins | 5 mins | REST | 15 mins | 10 mins | REST | 10 mins | 10 mins

Find and fetch keys

This skill means you'll never lose your keys again, even on walks. It is valuable training that builds on your dog's existing skills (see 'Find it!', Day 14; 'Fetch!', Day 17; and 'Hold', Day 18).

1 Attach a cloth item to a keyring containing a single spare key. Take care that your dog does not attempt to eat or swallow this. If this is the case, go back to 'Hold' (see page 59) for more practice first. You and your dog will play 'Find it!' (see page 51), 'Fetch!' (see page 56) and 'Hold' with this keyring.

2 Begin by hiding the keyring under objects and asking your dog to find and retrieve it. Always take the keyring from him and reward your dog with a toy or treat – never leave him to play with the keyring itself. Repeat five times, then rest.

3 Walk in a straight line with your dog at heel, then drop the keyring behind you. Send him back to find and fetch it. Repeat five times, keeping the 'Find it!' exciting and fun. On your walks, repeat from Step 1. Only switch to your real, everyday keys when you are both confident.

Stay – even when I disappear

This simple task will teach your dog to sit still when you go out of sight.

1 Ask your dog to 'Sit' and 'Stay'. Arrange him so that he is facing towards the direction in which you are going to walk away.

2 Step away from your dog and briefly pass behind a piece of furniture, then return. Praise and release your dog. Repeat four times, then step behind a doorway, return, praise, release as before. Repeat four times.

3 As you step behind the doorway, count to three, then return. Repeat, counting to five this time. Increase the time spent out of sight by only a few seconds at a time. After five goes, repeat – but only count to two seconds again before returning. Rest.

Socialization 6

Meeting new dogs

Do not allow your dog to lunge or stare at other dogs in a confrontational way. Keep him on a loose lead when greeting. If calm, allow a greeting. If he is excited, repeat your 'Come away' and 'Sit' training, offering frequent rewards to prevent frustration. Speak to him gently but keep the rules (stated above) clear and easy to follow. Never allow your dog to rush over to other dogs when off-lead.

People in uniform

High-visibility jackets, motorcycle helmets, heavy boots, and post bags can all be unnerving to a dog. Allow your dog to greet uniformed people and perhaps ask a postal worker if he or she could offer your dog a treat every time they visit. A great friendship can develop, so if the answer is 'yes', leave a pot of treats by your front door.

Day 20

Stay – even when I disappear (DAY 19)

SOCIALIZATION 6: Meeting new dogs (DAY 19)

Find and fetch keys (DAY 19)

Roll a ball

FREE CHOICE

Find a treat under a pot

10 mins   10 mins   5 mins   REST   5 mins   10 mins   REST   10 mins

Roll a ball

It's fun to teach your dog to nudge a ball into a goal, and good for his dexterity. The size of the ball can vary, so any type is suitable, but do choose one your dog cannot carry or puncture easily.

1 Place a treat near the ball, so that your dog has to push his nose slightly under the ball to reach it. Praise as he does so, and repeat five times.

2 Move the treat much closer to the ball so that your dog needs to move the ball out of the way to reach the treat. As he nudges the ball, say 'Push', and praise. Repeat five times until he is happily nosing the ball away.

3 Ask him to 'Push' without placing a treat. Wait, and try to allow him to work out what to do. As he searches for the treat (and nudges the ball), praise well and give him a treat yourself. Repeat until he confidently links 'Push' with the nudging action.

Free choice

You are nearly at the last day of the plan! Free choice is more important than ever, as you look back over all the knowledge you and your dog have gained. Today, pick your dog's favourite task, and go through it again at a simple level. He will be used to the interaction with you and this will be a reminder that training is low-pressure – or no-pressure, when it is enjoyable!

Plan for the future

List the things you still want to improve and match these to training tasks in the plan. Your dog may still be jumping up, for example, but now you have a huge choice of ways to replace this unwanted behaviour with one you prefer. Be creative. There are few limits!

Find a treat under a pot

This is a magic trick and search game all in one. Your dog will really enjoy hunting for a tasty treat by smell alone. It provides excellent stimulation for your dog's nose and entertainment for you both.

1 Place three plastic cups (or plastic flower pots) in a line. Allow your dog to watch you placing a treat under one of them.

2 Ask your dog to 'Find it!'. Allow him to sniff at the cups to locate the treat. Repeat this three times, then hide the treat while out of his sight. Repeat this three times.

3 Always allow your dog to tip over the chosen cup himself. His sense of smell will tell him where the treat is, but if you intervene he will wait for your signal instead. Finally, ask a helper to hide the treat so that you cannot influence him!

Day 21

Roll a ball
(DAY 20)

Find a treat
under a pot
(DAY 20)

CATCH!

Wave bye-bye

Take a bow

| 5 mins | 5 mins | REST | 10 mins | REST | 10 mins | 10 mins | REST & PLAY |

Wave bye-bye

Your dog has nearly completed his 21-Day Plan, so a wave brings this effort, and all those social interactions, to a fitting conclusion.

1 Sit your dog at heel, rather than in front of you, and ask him to 'Give a paw' (see page 44). Notice that you will need to reach your hand around your body to give the signal from this new angle. Repeat four times.

2 Hold your hand ready as if to take the paw but instead, say 'Wave!' as his paw lifts off the ground; immediately praise, and reward. Repeat four times, moving him off the spot each time, then back to the heel position.

3 Convert your hand gesture into a 'wave' as you give the command. Your aim is to ask your dog to wave to others in front of him, so he must remain at your side, facing forward towards your audience.

Catch!

Many dogs choose to wait until a flying item has dropped to the floor. Catch! teaches your dog to intercept the item in mid-air.

1 Hold a small treat in your hand above your dog's head. Keep it quite close to his muzzle as he looks up, then drop it directly above where his mouth is. Repeat until he begins to anticipate and grab the treat in mid-air. Say 'Catch!' as he does so.

2 Step away from him and toss the treat in an arc towards his muzzle. Keep your movements slow and steady, and make sure that he is closely following your hand. Once he is catching in this way, step further away and repeat. This may take some time as he learns to judge the speed and movement of the object. When he is catching this confidently, switch to an easy-to-catch toy.

Take a bow

Your 21-day effort deserves recognition, so this trick shows how you can both take a bow, hopefully to some well-deserved applause!

1 Begin with your dog in a 'Stand'. Hold a treat on his nose, then gradually lower the treat. Keep the treat very close to his nose, moving it inwards towards his body so that he drops his chin and shoulders to reach it.

2 Keep the treat moving so that your dog dips his nose down to his chest to reach it. Once he does so, say 'Bow'; praise and treat. Release and repeat five times. If necessary, place the back of your hand underneath and just in front of his back legs, to keep them off the ground.

3 As you say 'Bow', be sure to bow yourself, too – this becomes the body signal along with the command. Face a mirror, and both of you can take a bow. Congratulations! You have successfully completed the 21-Day Plan!

Part 3:
50 Quick Fixes

Fast and easy ways to solve tricky problems

How to use this section

The key to eradicating common problems lies in identifying the exact cause of the problem. Before you start troubleshooting any behaviours, examine the problem in exact detail. Also check that there are no safety or risk factors that may affect your attempts to help your dog.

Always address problems as soon as you can, rather than allowing errors to be repeated. This is important because practice makes behaviour permanent – whether it's desired or unwanted behaviour. Part of the troubleshooting process is accepting that although some troublesome behaviour is natural for your dog, it could contravene the law, so this is another reason to act early. You are responsible for your dog's behaviour no matter how suddenly it arises.

At all times, look out for your dog; never allow him to make a mistake that you could otherwise prevent. Prevention is better than re-training. If he does make a mistake, remember that harsh or physical punishment will always make a problem far worse and must be avoided.

Whose problem is it?

Start by listing any problems you are experiencing with your dog. Next to each problem, note where it occurs, to whom, and why you think your dog is doing it. What is your dog hoping to achieve by the way he is currently acting? Decide whether any item on your list is a normal dog behaviour that is just occurring in the wrong place or at the wrong time. For example, digging is normal and enjoyable for dogs, but the problem lies with where he chooses to dig and the mess he creates!

Behaviour with no obvious cause or target, such as spinning or obsessive tail-chasing, is a more complex issue. If you are concerned, ask your vet to refer your dog to a clinical behaviourist.

Assess the risk level of behaviour

Does the problem behaviour put you, your dog, or someone else at risk? If so, how high is that risk? If the risk is low, such as a puppy nibbling at table legs, you can deal with this gently and gradually with patience and training. An example of a medium-risk problem would be a small dog who jumps up in a friendly way but could knock a small child over – here you would need to use a combination of removing access at times and using training for the long term. High-risk behaviours, such as a large, fast dog lunging at traffic, or a dog who causes damage to himself or property when left alone, require immediate measures; these must be strictly maintained while you teach your dog or seek professional guidance.

Plan before you start

All the troubleshooting advice in this section combines training, environmental changes, and practical management. Plan ahead using the same step-by-step approach advocated in the 21-Day Plan. Decide on an acceptable and realistic outcome. If you feel out of your depth, seek professional help.

1: Mouthing

Young puppies use their mouths to explore fingers, clothing, toys, and in fact most objects! Normal canine play also includes mouthing. Your puppy will naturally grow out of this in time.

- Establish some 'human rules'. Mouthing must only be very gentle and if it is not, stop interacting with him immediately.
- Provide suitable, tasty chew toys and swap these for whatever he is chewing. Stay calm.
- If the mouthing is persistent, place him in his bed for a nap, as he is probably overtired or overstimulated.
- If an older dog is mouthing, this may be caused by frustration, fear, or dislike at being handled. Teach him that what's upsetting him is actually enjoyable by offering him food that he likes or by stroking him calmly at the same time.

2: Frustration

If your dog is unable to achieve an expected outcome immediately, he may become frustrated. Frustration is demonstrated by jumping up, snatching, lunging, and barking. Any simple training exercise in the 21-Day Plan will help your dog to deal with impatience as he learns how to work his way towards a goal step by step.

- Teach him to sit calmly at a good distance at times when he would rather lunge or bark, then reward him well.
- Use 'Come away' so that he turns away and pays attention to you instead.
- Encourage him to behave calmly around people and other dogs using thorough socialization (see pages 25, 33, 37, 41, 53, and 61).
- Teach your dog to 'Fetch' and 'Give' using toys; this will stop him from snatching.

3: Barking in the garden

Dogs have excellent hearing and will alert you to noises they find unsettling or exciting by barking. Outdoor settings provide wider opportunities for sounds to travel, but scent travels further too – particularly that of a female dog in season. This can frustrate male dogs and cause them to bark frantically.

If you know your dog barks frequently when outdoors, do not leave him there, as the barking can quickly become a noise nuisance. Allow your dog into your garden only when you are there to call him away from sounds. If he does not come immediately, use a long lead or line to draw him towards you for a reward. Keep the lead attached for all garden visits until he returns to you reliably.

4: Hyperactivity

Active breeds require a great deal of mental and physical exercise and this must be provided several times daily. If you are unable to do this, your dog is likely to suffer from excess energy at home.

● Check that your dog is not on a high-energy diet, and reduce high-energy treats and snacks in line with advice from your vet.
● Dogs can behave hyperactively when they are in a high-stress situation. Whenever this is the case, remove your dog to a calm, quiet place where he can settle.
● Never shout, as this adds to the agitation. Teach your dog to settle using 'Down' and 'Stay' instead.

5: Unmotivated or not listening

Your dog may look or move away when you are trying to teach him. He is not being stubborn – he may just be uninterested in the reward on offer. Ensure that the reward is of sufficiently high value (strongly scented, soft food such as chicken, ham, or cheese may be a better option than dry biscuit). Or he may not be hungry, so make the treats smaller and teach your dog before meals rather than afterwards. Consider offering a soft toy that you can move around as a reward instead. Alternatively, he may be feeling under pressure and is looking away to avoid conflict or unwanted attention. If you think this is the case, end the training session and allow him to rest. Make the next session much simpler and allow your dog to earn some easy rewards at first.

6: Fear and stress signals

Stress signs are often misinterpreted as 'disobedience' or 'dominance' when in fact they are clear signals that a dog is afraid or trying to avoid something. They are often made as a warning to you or other dogs.

● Looking away, licking lips, stiffening of body and yawning are all stress signs, so you need to be aware of their appearance when interacting with your dog.
● Stress signals can rapidly escalate into more serious behaviour, because he is showing that he cannot cope. If you spot one, immediately intervene by calling your dog away from whatever situation he is in; ask him to sit near you or allow him to retreat to his bed to calm down.

50 Quick Fixes

7: Environmental distractions

Your dog may find some environments challenging and difficult to cope with. Noisy building work, parks with other dogs, and busy roads can cause a lack of concentration. In these situations, give him something simple and familiar to do, such as 'Sit' – 'Stay' for a few seconds. Reward him well, then move him away from the distraction. Gradually increase the number of environmental distractions and ask him to focus on you by training simple tasks throughout. Socialize him more thoroughly in these environments over the next few weeks so that he becomes used to them as part of everyday life.

8: Socializing with strangers

Your dog may be very good at recognizing family members but bark or avoid strangers, particularly children or people wearing glasses or in uniform. If so, remedial socialization is essential. Take a bag of tasty, scented food such as chicken or cheese with you when you take him on walks. Only go to places where you (and he) can clearly see people approaching. When you see a person nearby, praise your dog and offer him some food, keeping him at a distance from the person at first. Repeat until you see your dog happily look at you when a person appears. Seek professional help if your dog shows any signs of aggression towards people.

9: Firework and noise fears

Your dog may be sensitive to certain sounds such as fireworks, aeroplanes, or household appliances (vacuum cleaners and lawnmowers are common culprits). Sound sensitivity can be hereditary or may develop from a single, frightening event.

● Never force your dog to be close to noises that he finds unpleasant. Instead, record the sound and play it at a very low volume while your dog is doing something he really enjoys, such as eating or playing.
● Gradually increase the volume over a period of weeks, always pairing it with a fun activity, so that he becomes accustomed to the sound and associates it with enjoyment.
● Make sure your dog has a place to retreat to when loud noises are expected, and seek professional help if you are concerned.

10: Destructive chewing

Your dog may simply be exploring with his mouth (see page 68), especially during puppyhood and adolescence, when he will also be teething. An older dog may chew for comfort or stress release. Provide him with strong but tasty dog chews such as hollow rubber toys with a scrape of cheese spread or meat paste inside. Dog puzzle toys in which his dinner can be placed can help occupy and distract a dog, helping him to enjoy foraging and fulfilling his natural prey instinct.

Boredom causes destructive behaviour, so give your dog plenty of stimulation. Do not leave him alone for more than four hours per day. If you need to be away for longer than this, use dog daycare or employ a dog sitter.

50 Quick Fixes

11: Separation anxiety

Some dogs find it hard to cope alone or when separated from a family member. Your dog needs to learn gradually how to cope without the person or other dog to whom he is attached. Make sure he has plenty of enjoyment and time with others, and that he has a safe place for retreat when he does need to be left alone. A dog that does not like to be left alone is not a suitable pet for a family who are regularly away from home. For most cases of separation or isolation distress, seeking referral to a clinical behaviourist is a priority.

12: Chasing animals on walks

If your dog likes to hunt and chase, it must be controlled. Dogs are not only capable of chasing toys but also creatures, such as cats, squirrels, and even horses. Strict laws apply to dog owners regarding the chasing of sheep and livestock, and you will be heavily penalized should this occur.

Teach your dog a rock-solid recall command, a 'Sit' (or 'Down') and 'Stay', and keep him on a lead or line anywhere where livestock or other animals may be running loose. Control his chasing of toys at first and gradually increase the intensity and speed until your dog will ignore even the fastest-moving live temptation.

13: Pulling on the lead

If your dog pulls at the lead, he may be trying to reach others, to sniff or explore, or to run ahead of you. He is pulling you, often quite hard, to get to where he would like to go!

● Check that you are not winding the lead tightly around your hand or wrist. Let it stay loose and steer your dog near to your feet.
● Only step forward when the lead is slack. If your dog dives forward again, take a pace or two back, reposition him at your feet and relax the lead again.
● Never move forward on a tight lead. Your dog will quickly learn that a tight lead means he will be moved back to the start point. A slack lead means he can move forward. He must learn to watch your movement, to make sure he stays by your feet.

14: Jumping up

Greeting new people is an exciting event for a dog, and even puppies quickly learn that faces are the centre of human communication and information. As a result, they sometimes jump up to reach this interesting place. Teach your dog that to be allowed to say hello, he must first sit and remain sitting. If he moves, instruct the person to ignore him. Keep him on a lead so that he cannot make physical contact with the person. Your dog will quickly realize that to greet someone, he must sit and wait for the person to come to him.

50 Quick Fixes

15: Guarding food and toys

Create a relaxed attitude around items by teaching your dog to swap them for better things. Never simply take food or toys away from him without replacing them immediately with something better. Teach 'Fetch!' and 'Give' to establish the rules about items and be generous with rewards when your dog gives items to you. Call him to you away from toys and items, rather than going towards him to take them away. If your dog guards toys using aggression, stiffens up when someone passes him while he is eating, or shows seemingly unpredictable reactions when food is present, ask your vet for referral to a qualified behaviourist.

16: Gobbling food

Does your dog vacuum his dinner up in seconds? If so, check with your vet in case this presents a health risk. To slow things down, hide his food inside foraging or puzzle toys. Scatter kibble in the garden to encourage him to hunt for it, or save some of it and use it for training later in the day. Be aware that dogs who like to gobble their food may see it as highly valuable and have a tendency to guard (see above).

17: House soiling

Toileting outdoors does not always come naturally. If your dog is regularly soiling inside the house, he needs more guidance. Is he choosing a regular location to toilet indoors, such as a soft surface or a quiet corner? If he chooses a mat by the door, replace this with an absorbent puppy pad or paper that you can then move outside. Dogs usually toilet after meals, drinking, and playing, and upon waking.

A clear routine and supervision are essential. Watch your dog closely for signs that he may need to toilet and take him regularly, using the same route where possible, to the outside toilet area you have chosen. Reward him using treats and enthusiastic praise when he succeeds.

18: Fence guarding

Patrolling sections of the garden, or a front window within the home, causes frustration, barking, and sometimes aggression. You also need to be aware that one day your dog may get through the window or around the fence to reach a passer-by; this is an obvious risk. Teach your dog to come to you from the fence or window the minute you see him begin to target it. Reduce his unsupervised access to this area and make sure the boundary is secure. Do not give visitors free access to the garden unless your dog knows them well.

19: Fighting with other dogs

Not all dogs get on well. Is your dog squabbling over possessions or places, does he dislike specific dogs, or is he worried about other dogs in general?

● If he is fighting over possessions, control all access to these yourself and teach your dog to give objects to you willingly.
● A fearful dog needs gradual exposure to friendly dogs to build his confidence and you may need expert help to achieve this.
● If dogs within your home are fighting, use the 21-Day Plan to establish clearer boundaries and better control.

If the aggressive behaviour has caused injury, or if you fear that it might on another occasion, seek professional help immediately.

20: Running away

Your dog may find it more interesting to explore his surroundings or other people than to return to you. Teach 'Come', but also use a 10 m (30 ft) long line when taking your dog for walks. At several points along each walk, back away from your dog and call him happily to you. Reward him with treats, praise, and a game, then make him wait until you release him so that he can go exploring again. Repeat this frequently on walks and use the line to insist he returns if there is hesitation. He will gradually learn to return to you regardless of any distractions you encounter.

21: Stealing items and food

Dogs find it hard to resist food or any interesting items placed within their reach. If you have puppies, keep valuable items well out of the way and encourage children to tidy away their toys, as puppies tend to explore – and chew – a great deal. Dogs that can reach work surfaces need careful supervision, because once they have reached one valuable food item they will always look for another. Teach your dog to come to you for a treat, calling him away from valuable items rather than snatching them away from him. Above all, do not chase your dog to retrieve stolen items as it quickly develops into an unwanted game.

22: Grabbing the post

Dogs become very excitable when letters arrive in the post. Novel objects mysteriously appear through a small gap in the door at the same time each day! Your dog may shake them or tear them, and this can be a costly problem. Prevent your dog from having free access to the letterbox by fitting a cage on the rear of the door or providing an external letterbox. Break the habit by teaching your dog to move away from the door and do not allow him to patrol this area at times when deliveries are expected.

23: Car travel problems

Cars are noisy, smelly, and move without warning. Dogs often travel in the rear, away from their owners who could be a source of comfort. If your dog is unhappy about car travel, first assess if he is suffering from nausea; he may not actually vomit but may drool. Ask your vet for assistance if nausea is a problem.

You can change your dog's feelings about car travel by providing a cosy bed and meals for him in the vehicle when it is stationary, starting the engine only when he is settled. Take a passenger with you who can distract and play gently with him, so he learns to associate cars with a pleasant experience. Move the vehicle only a short distance at first, then slowly increase journey times, to help build his enjoyment and trust.

24: Refusal to walk

If your dog has no medical problems, refusal to walk is usually avoidance or fear-related. A young puppy may freeze when met with the uncertainty of being outdoors or he may dislike the feeling of a collar and lead. If this is the case, allow your puppy to wear his collar when at home and attach his lead when supervised so that he can just trail it around until he is accustomed to the sensation. When out with your dog, do not pull the lead to encourage him to walk, as he will automatically pull against a tight lead – it will cause him to feel trapped. Take treats and toys with you to encourage him and play with him along his walk, perhaps stopping to reassure him from time to time.

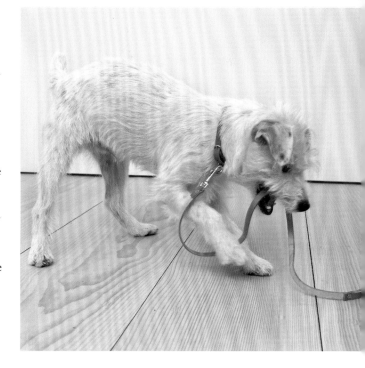

25: Digging

Dogs dig for fun, to explore, and to stash items for later enjoyment. Digging is a normal behaviour but it creates a great deal of mess and can damage precious shrubs and lawns. Place favourite plants in large or tall pots that he is less able to reach. Supervise your dog closely in the garden but be careful not to create an attention-getting game.

- Provide him with a suitable digging area surrounded by slabs, to make sweeping the earth back a simple task. Bury rubber toys and other items in this digging pit.
- When your dog aims for other parts of the garden, call him to his digging area.
- If he returns to the unwanted area, put a lead or line on him to insist he moves away.

26: Dashing out of the door

Doors can become a trigger for dogs to dive for the opening – it represents a chance to explore the outside world or to greet arriving visitors. However, excitement around the door is rarely useful and it can lead some dogs to become defensive. Practise your dog's door skills by asking him to sit calmly near the door, then open and close the door several times, while he waits for a reward without moving. Then ask a family member to stand outside the door and repeat the training, allowing the family member to enter only when your dog sits calmly. Keep your dog on a lead throughout this training for additional safety.

50 Quick Fixes

27: Cats and other pets

Dogs naturally hunt and chase small moving items and this may create problems with other pets, especially cats that can come and go freely. With a resident cat, introduce your dog carefully and prevent him from chasing by keeping him on a lead and calling him to you every time the cat is present. Reward both pets with tasty treats in each other's presence. With smaller pets, such as rabbits, do not allow your dog to stalk them or stare into their cages. Call him away. Do not allow the animals free access to one another until you are certain both can stay calm, as they can seriously injure one another.

28: Fear of children

Children move quickly, tend to stare, and often make loud, high-pitched noises. These can all be quite startling for a dog. Socialize your puppy well with children by providing lots of opportunities for them to enjoy supervised time together. Coach children to behave appropriately around your dog and explain to them that dogs do not enjoy hugging or being disturbed when resting. An older dog will need careful teaching if he is afraid of children, using play and tasty food to build positive experiences. If your dog shows any aggression, seek professional help.

29: Aggressive behaviour

Aggression is your dog's way of communicating that he is uncomfortable, frightened, or wants something to stop or move away. Dogs only choose aggression as a last resort. It is not the sign of a confident dog, no matter how he may appear. Look for stress indicators (see page 70) and distract him before they escalate. Any form of punishment will rapidly worsen aggressive behaviour. Aggression is best dealt with using kind, professional guidance from a qualified behaviourist. Ask your vet to check your dog's health, too, as this often contributes to aggressive behaviour.

30: Dislikes grooming

Groom your dog on a regular basis, using treats to create an enjoyable association with handling and restraint. Always use gentle, soft brushes to tidy up his coat and keep all grooming sessions very short. Even if you brush only a small area of your dog's coat each day, you will find that over a week or so it will be fully cared for. In the same way, using nail clippers only one nail at a time over a period of days, and rewarding well as you do so, will give your dog a positive experience.

Clean his teeth using tasty toothpaste designed for dogs – this may help him accept this valuable treatment.

31: Boisterous play

Some dogs become very excitable during play but this can deteriorate into squabbles if left to escalate. If your dog is boisterous with people, particularly children, do not allow uncontrolled meetings. Teach your dog that play sessions end at the earliest sign of rough or careless behaviour. Call him away from other dogs or people after a short play period, allowing him to return when calm. This becomes a self-rewarding habit; calm behaviour permits play, and overexcitement causes play to stop.

Do not allow a puppy to repeatedly pester an older dog. Give the older dog a place to retreat to and occupy the puppy with other games.

32: Eating faeces

Dogs scavenge for and often eat anything they find interesting. A dog that eats his own faeces or those of other animals may need a veterinary check to ensure there are no digestive issues. Although this habit appears revolting to humans, far more serious problems can arise from an owner's reaction to the behaviour. Avoid punishing your dog and stay calm. Call him to you, rewarding him when he obeys.

Teach a solid retrieve for any and all items he may eat, starting with large toys that he cannot consume, so that he brings them to you instead of swallowing them. You may need to muzzle your dog or keep him on a lead to prevent him eating potentially harmful items. If the problem continues, seek professional guidance.

33: Older dogs, slower learning

An older dog needs additional consideration when training. He may learn more slowly and may not remember skills unless he has opportunities for plenty of repetition. Recognize that his health and senses are declining and take extra care not to startle him. Old dogs do not just 'slow down' or become stubborn when you are walking or training them. If this seems to be the case, it is likely that he is in pain or he is attempting to see or hear better.

Ask your vet to check for signs of cognitive decline. Behavioural symptoms include confusion, night waking, separation anxiety, and 'forgetful' house soiling. If this is the case, ask your vet to refer you to a registered behaviourist for help.

34: Mounting

Male and female dogs indulge in mounting, which is a form of sexual behaviour and rarely harmful. They can mount beds, cushions, other pets and people. When your dog is about to mount, distract him and move him away. Give him something to play with or chew, or allow him to mount his own toys. Attach a lead to his collar if controlling him is difficult. Move him away for a few minutes to allow him to become calm. Make sure that you provide him with plenty of other activities on which to expend his energy. Ask your vet for advice regarding castration of a male dog, as this may help reduce mounting activity.

50 Quick Fixes

35: Older dog with a younger dog

A younger dog can cause disruption for an older dog even if they are to become good friends. Older dogs have learned their home routine and space. Younger dogs do not have impulse control; they snatch toys, play roughly, and occupy family attention.

An older dog is likely to feel insecure about a new arrival. Make sure each dog has a quiet space to rest. Give your older dog plenty of one-to-one attention, occasionally taking him for walks by himself as before. Do not allow the younger dog to pester him, and make certain there are no reasons for the dogs to compete over food or toys.

36: Moving house

Dogs enjoy routine, so moving house can be a stressful disturbance. Aim for a smooth transition by allowing your dog to retreat to his bed while you pack up household belongings. Arrange for him to stay with a friend or family while the move is in progress, or use kennels. Once you are settled in, take your dog on a familiar walk before bringing him to his new home. Set up his bed in a quiet, cosy space and give him his favourite meals for a few days. Look out for scent-marking behaviour and any lapse in toilet training; quickly distract your dog if this begins to occur. Keep all other routines as familiar as possible.

37: Creating a safe haven

Dogs benefit from having a safe place to retreat to during times of stress or worry. A haven or den helps alleviate anxiety, whether this is caused by loud noises, such as fireworks, or separation issues. Create a haven for your dog by providing a quiet zone, with cosy bedding, water, and some tasty chew toys.

A crate may be suitable, as you can insulate the walls, ceiling, and floor to block sound. Feed him meals and stroke him in his haven; make it a calm, enjoyable resting space. If trained successfully, your dog will choose to relax there rather than feel he is forced to cope with challenging situations.

38: Fear of the outdoors

Your dog – especially if he is a puppy – may pull towards home and appear frantic in his efforts to retrace his steps. Or he may only want to walk on a familiar route, pulling insistently towards that familiar direction. He may avoid certain objects on the walk, such as plastic bags, rubbish bins, or houses that clearly contain other dogs.

If this is the case, mix some extra-tasty food with his dinner and place a line of it in the direction your dog previously avoided, so that he eats the pieces one by one. Praise him well, and repeat. Keep the lead slack. If your dog is too stressed to eat, choose shorter and quieter routes at first.

50 Quick Fixes

39: Refusing to eat

If you have any concerns about your dog's weight, check it with your vet and make sure your dog's diet is appropriate for his age and activity level. Keep a diary of what he eats and when. You may find that he is eating more than you imagine. If he is otherwise healthy, don't worry if he occasionally eats less or refuses a meal. Never try to encourage your dog to eat by adding tastier food, as he will learn that by refusing some food, you will produce a better option! Stay relaxed; if your dog does not wish to eat, calmly remove the bowl after about ten minutes and do not offer food again until the next mealtime.

40: Begging at the dinner table

Dogs quickly learn that food is available at the dinner table, and that people often share it! Unfortunately, it only takes one tasty reward to teach your dog that this is a profitable hobby. For good table manners, you need to teach your dog to lie down and stay a little way from the table. Reward him by tossing treats from a separate, dog-proof treat pot, rather than feeding him from plates. Provide him with a tasty chew to further encourage him to lie down and relax. If visitors insist on sharing their food with him, provide them with a side plate 'for the dog'. If you wish, you can then offer this to him later, well away from the table.

41: Walking with pushchairs and mobility scooters

Walking your dog next to a wheeled object may cause him to become entangled or to pull away, causing it to tip over. Teach him to stay close without becoming afraid or unsettled. Begin by moving the wheels forward a little and encourage him to follow, holding a treat in the hand nearest to him. Repeat until he confidently follows you each time the wheels move forward. Increase the distance, step by step, keeping the motion smooth. Once he is confident, steer the wheels in a gentle semicircle in the direction away from him, encouraging him to follow. Curve gently back again, taking care not to trap his paws. With practice, he will confidently follow the movement.

42: Street safety

If your dog behaves in an unsettled manner in the street, this can be a risk to both of you and to other people. Teach your dog to sit at the kerb and keep him close to you when others pass by.

If your dog lunges at people, other dogs, or vehicles, keep him at a distance from them and teach him to sit calmly for a treat instead. Anticipate that children may want to approach and stroke your dog – and some may do so without asking. Socialize him well to all these situations and keep interactions light, fun, and brief. He will learn that they are just part of normal life and not targets for uncontrolled play.

50 Quick Fixes

43: Keeping within the law

Dogs' behaviour can be unexpected. Make yourself aware of the laws appertaining to dogs, including control in private, in public, and animal welfare laws. You are responsible for your dog's behaviour and wellbeing. If problems arise, you may find that the law is not sympathetic if your dog could have been better trained or controlled. Avoid situations you suspect could be potentially risky for your dog, and seek help with aggression towards people, dogs, or livestock. Always pick up after your dog has toileted and dispose of any waste hygienically.

44: Barking at other dogs

Dogs often bark when meeting each other on walks. Some dogs are more vocal than others and a bark can signify many emotions. Which dogs does yours bark at? Note how close he needs to be before he begins, and how long it takes him to settle. It may be that he has not had enough positive social experience with other dogs to enable him to stay calm. Begin by finding a calm adult dog, and aim to introduce your dog over a number of walks. Once he has learned that he can go for walks and greet a familiar dog calmly, you can use this same approach to encourage calm interactions with other dogs.

45: Not fetching toys

If your dog tends to refuse to return to you with a toy, teach him to fetch by tossing the toy into a corner of a room, so that he has to turn back to you once he has possession. Outside, keep him on his lead to prevent him dashing past, but aim to swap the toy for another or even a treat, rather than simply snatching at it when you're taking it back from him. Make his final reward another game of fetch. If your dog is simply not interested in fetching toys, choose soft, squeaky toys and hide food inside. Play with your dog at times when he is most active, such as first thing in the morning.

46: Biting at clothing

Playing puppies often grab and pull at clothing, particularly sleeves and trouser legs. If this happens, calmly disentangle your dog's mouth from the item and offer a more suitable toy to play with. Use a lead or house line to move him away and provide plenty of rewards when he resists temptation. Older dogs that bite at clothing must learn the 'Off' command (see page 35). Do not allow uncontrolled games of tug with toys unless your dog releases items immediately on command. Such games must have clearly defined rules for them to be safe, as it is often this uncontrolled impulse that causes your dog to tug at items in the first place.

47: Growling

Growling can sometimes be in play, but it can threaten something more serious. Always heed growling and immediately put a stop to whatever seems to be causing his growling reaction. Do not follow advice stating that growling should be punished or 'dominated'. This is likely to escalate into a serious bite. Review what caused your dog to growl, as it will usually be something he was attempting to avoid or prevent, and it is often a sign of low confidence. If your dog growls over objects or at people, seek professional assistance without delay.

48: Finding a good training class

Training methods have changed to become kind, fair, and more effective than they used to be; there is no room for harsh punishment in the name of dog training or behaviour modification. Visit several training classes in your area and reject any that favour the use of choke chains, prongs, or shock collars. Clicker training is an option, but it is not essential. Look for reward-based methods and relaxed dogs in small classes, of no more than 6–8 dogs per class. Check that the trainer is experienced with all breeds and ages of dog, and ask whether they are registered with any known associations. This provides you with security and confidence in the case of any queries or complaints. There are now many qualifications a trainer can achieve, so ask about these too.

50 Quick Fixes

49: Dislike of harness, collar, or lead

Your dog may be excited about walks, but when you try to put on his harness, collar, or lead, he runs and hides. This may be because he has worn one previously that was uncomfortable, but more often it is simply because dogs react badly to unfamiliar items going over their heads or restraining them around the neck. Sound-sensitive dogs often tend to dislike the jangling noise that metal attachments such as clips can make.

Several times each day, get out the walking equipment, but don't try to put it on him – simply offer him treats as you bring it out, then put the equipment away. After a few days, practise putting the harness/collar/lead onto him and teach him to enjoy this experience by using tasty food every time. Don't rush: train your dog to remain calmly sitting or standing while you get him ready, and reward him well.

50: Fear of the vet

Even if you have taken your dog to the vet regularly when he was young, a single stressful event at the surgery may create a learned dislike of visiting it.

To get around this problem:
● Ask your vet if you can bring your dog at times when you do not actually require a visit.
● Check when the surgery is quiet and aim for these times.
● Play 'visit the vet' at home, with plenty of goodies to reward your dog for calm behaviour while you examine him all over.
● Note when regular vet appointments are due (such as for vaccinations) and practise the suggestions above every day for several weeks prior to your visit.
● You may be able to request a specific vet if your dog appears to have a preference. If so, take advantage of this kind offer.

Socialization progress chart

Make sure your dog experiences all of the following, preferably every week. Reward calm, happy behaviour with attention, treats, and cuddles. If he shows signs of uncertainty, reassure gently and stay calm. Distract a puppy with a delicious treat or a toy and give him a little more distance next time. Use the right-hand columns to tick off (or date) sessions.

TASKS	Number of repeats		
Getting used to people			
Adult men and women			
Elderly people			
Delivery people			
Joggers			
People in uniform			
People in glasses and sunglasses			
Teenagers			
Children (babies, toddlers, and older children)			
Getting used to other animals			
Puppies – quiet/noisy/bouncy			
Dog – dark coat/light coat/large/small			
Cats/Small pets			
Deer/Cows/Horses/Sheep			
Dealing with different environments			
Parks, shops, cafés, pubs			
School (outside, and always on lead)			
Busy road (always on lead)			
Vet, groomer, boarding kennels			

In and around transport			
Cars/lorries/vans/motorcycles/buses			
Familiarity with all sorts of surfaces			
Smooth/shiny/tiled floors			
Grass/gravel/sand			
Being alone or with strangers			
In a crate or room alone			
Lead held by stranger			
Happy to be handled			
Head/ears/teeth/paws			
Lift onto table/gentle restraint			
Unfazed by startling sounds			
Hairdryer/vacuum/washing machine			
Fridge/dishwasher/central heating/air conditioning			
Hot-air balloon/aeroplane/lawnmower			
Telephone/doorbell/answer machine			
Firework noise			
Other barking dogs			

Going forward

Your dog may need extensive practice in some of the situations listed here, as well as other aspects of his lifestyle. Draw up a continuation chart like this in a notebook to keep track of when you and he worked on those skills that need extra practice. Notice which ones he learns more quickly or more slowly, and always consider how you might be able to help him learn more easily.

Index

Acknowledgements

Picture credits

Every effort has been made to contact copyright holders. However, the publishers will be glad to rectify in future editions any inadvertent omissions brought to their attention.

All photographs are by Russell Sadur for Octopus Publishing Group Ltd, with the exception of the following additional material.
Alamy Blickwinkel 47al
Fotolia Cbckchristine 61b
Getty Images Flickr 79a; GK Hart/Vikki Hart 68b; Stephen Errico 5
Octopus Publishing Group Ltd 10, 70a, 73a, 88b; Adrian Pope 29a, 33bl, 37a, 39al, 74a; Mugford 13, 19, 69a, 71a; Tom Miles 45b, 63a, 77b
Shutterstock Andrzej Mielcarek 76b; Anna Hoychuk 11; bikeriderlondon 53a; Darlush M 86b; dogboxstudio 71b; Eric Isselee 85a, 87b, 90; Eric Lam 84a; Fly dragonfly 91b; Holbox 15l; Javier Brosch 75b; Naten 59a; Okssi 81a; Ratikova 80a; Warren Goldswain 15r; WilleeCole 87a; Yellowj 83b
Thinkstock Anders TÃ¥nger 17l; André Weyer 21l; BananaStock 14; Bojan Sokolovic 68a; Chris Amaral 2–3 & 86a, 78a; EmiliaU 81b; Frenk Kaufmann 16l; Hans Paulsson 85b; Fuse 82a, 88a; Kane Skennar 55b, 69b; Maciej Pokora 31a; Michael Blann 78b; Mustang 79, 84b; Odeon16 4; Ryhor Bruyeu 70b; Shanna Hendrickson 37b; Simone Van den berg 75a; Smithore 89; Stockbyte 73b; WilleeCole 74b; Zhenikeyev 18; Zoonar 17r

Author's acknowledgements

Thank you Amy, Louis, and to Martin Gadd for all their support.

Publisher's acknowledgements

Thank you to Emma-Clare Dunnett of www. puppyschool.co.uk for helping us to find puppies for the photoshoot. Thank you to all the owners and dogs who took part: Amanda Blatch and Buddy, Sarah Everett and Fudge, Amanda Harding and Pepe, Wendy Herat and Willow, Sharon Hynes and Loki, and to our author Karen Wild for kindly bringing her own dogs, Bonnie and Pickles. Thanks to Vicky and Maggie at Zownir Locations Ltd for providing a beautiful apartment for the photoshoot (www.zownirlocations.com). Thank you to Pets Corner (www.petscorner.co.uk) for their help with supplying props and petcare items. And lastly, many thanks to Russell Sadur and his assistant Stuart Milne for the photography.

Editorial Director: **Trevor Davies**
Production Controller: **Sarah Connelly**
Picture Researcher: **Giulia Hetherington**

Produced for Octopus Publishing Group Ltd by Tracy Killick Art Direction and Design
Project Editor: **Sarah Tomley**
Art Director: **Tracy Killick**
Proof Reader: **Louise Abbott**
Indexer: **Hilary Bird**